Giles Gossip
Coronation Anecdotes

Gossip, Giles

Coronation Anecdotes

ISBN/EAN: 978-3-86741-318-3
First published in 2010 by Europaeischer Hochschulverlag GmbH & Co KG, Bremen, Germany.

© Europaeischer Hochschulverlag GmbH & Co KG, Fahrenheitstr. 1, D-28359 Bremen (www.ehv-online.com). All rights reserved.

This book is a reproduction of an out of print title and has originally been published in 1823. Because no electronic master copies of this title could be obtained, the publisher had to reuse old copies of the text. We therefore apologize for any possible loss in quality.

Giles Gossip

Coronation Anecdotes

Contents

§ 1. Anecdotes of the Regalia and Royal Vestments   1

§ 2. Anecdotes of the Disused Ceremonies of the Coronation.   14

§ 3. Anecdotes of the Assistant Offices of the Coronation.   29

§ 4. Anecdotes of the Actual Ceremonies of the Coronation,   45

    Coronation of his most excellent Majesty King George IV.   90

    Procession with, and Delivery of, the Regalia.   93

    Procession to the Abbey.   95

    Order.   96

    The Regalia.   101

    The King.   103

    Entrance into Westminster Abbey.   105

    The Recognition.   106

    The first Oblation.   106

    The Sermon.   109

    The Oath.   112

    The Anointing.   113

    The Presenting of the Spurs and Word, and the Girding and Oblation oft he Said Sword.   116

    The Investing with the Armill & Royal Robe, and the Delivery of the Orb.   117

    The Investiture per Annulum et Baculum.   118

    The Putting on of the Crown.   119

    The Presenting of the Holy Bible.   120

    The Benedicton, and Te Deum.   121

The Inthronization.	123
The Homage.	124
The Communion.	126
The Exhortation.	128
The General Confession.	128
The Absolution.	129
The Prayer of Address.	130
The Prayer of Consecration.	130
The Final Prayers.	132
The Recess.	133
Return of the Procession to the Hall.	134
The King,	140
The Banquet.	143
The Challenge.	144
Proclamaton of the Styles.	147
Second Course.	147
Services in Pursuance of Claims.	147
The Platform.	151
Coronaton Galleries.	151
Westminster Hall.	152
Her Majesty's Protest Against the Decision of the Privy Council.	172
Footnotes	**184**

"In pensive thought recal the fancied scene,
See *Coronations* rise on every green." — Pope.

Advertisement.

The coronation of our monarchs presents a wide field of meditation to an intelligent eye. It is an epitome of the genius of the monarchy, and a miniature exhibition of the leading events of our annals.

Connected, in point of fact, with the first establishment of Christianity in this island, it also perpetuates some of the earliest British notions of public liberty; and while it confirms the hereditary claims of each succeeding prince, it is introduced by a recognition of some of the most ancient rights of the people,

> "Mighty states, *characterless*, are grated
> To dusty nothing,"

says that great dramatist who has so largely alluded to English coronations in his historical plays. These ceremonies exhibit the character of each constituent portion of the political body from age to age; and are chiefly valuable, perhaps, as preserving a chain of *national identity*, unbroken by conquest, or by civil war; by changing dynasties, or the most important revolutions of the empire: on the other hand, they present to us a vast *variety* of character and events.—They are associated with the gloom, "the dim religious light" of Anglo-Saxon history, with the stormy character of the Conquest and the Norman domination; they bring before us the lofty Plantagenet, the proud Tudor, and the tyrannical but unfortunate House of Stuart, in all the pomp, and strife, and vanity of their respective pretensions.

But the general reader will require a *clue* to this symbolical kind of instruction: a companion to his recollections of such an exhibition, which, without destroying the vividness and pleasure of the pageantry, shall connect its objects with the march of history, the advance of civilization, and the final settlement of our laws and liberties. "To converse with historians," says an accomplished writer, "is always to keep good company;" while, "to carry back the mind *in uniting* and to make it old," is the one great difficulty which Lord Bacon points out in the study of history. Every effort, therefore, to smooth this difficult path, and to introduce the rising generation to such company, will be properly appreciated by the anxious and intelligent parent; and such is the design of this little volume. It is the especial business of the historian, certainly, to instruct; but the more he can keep alive our *interest* without flattering either our passions or vices, the more effectually will he accomplish his great object, and swell the train of the votaries of truth.

§ 1. Anecdotes of the Regalia and Royal Vestments

"History—the picture of man—has shared the fate of its original. It has had its infancy of *Fable*; its youth of Poetry; its manhood of Thought, Intelligence, and Reflection."—Anon.

No. 1. *The Regal Chair.*

The Regalia of England are the symbols of a monarchical authority that has been transmitted by coronation ceremonies for upwards of ten centuries. But the incorporation of England, Scotland, and Ireland, into one united kingdom,—an event peculiar to the coronation of George IV, to have recognised,—has connected the history of the Imperial Regalia with some tales of legendary lore, the truth of which, if this circumstance does not demonstrate, be assured, gentle reader, nothing will. Irish records are said to add at least another thousand years of substantial history to the honours of that solid regal seat, or coronation chair, in which our monarchs are both anointed and crowned [1]: while some of our own "honest chroniclers" assign to it a still more marvellous antiquity.

Holinshed gives us the history of one Gathelus, a Greek, who brought from Egypt into Spain the identical stone on which the patriarch Jacob slept and "poured oil" at Luz. He was "the sonne of Cecrops, who builded the citie of Athens;" but having married Scota, the daughter of Pharaoh, he resided for some time in Egypt, from whence he was induced to remove into the West by the judgments pronounced on that country by Moses. In Spain, "having peace with his neighbors, he builded a citie called Brigantia (Compostella)," where he "sat vpon his marble stone, gave lawes, and ministred justice vnto his people, thereby to maintaine them in wealth and quietnesse," And "Hereof it came to passe, that first in Spaine, after in Ireland, and then in Scotland, the kings which ruled over the Scotishmen received the crowne sittinge vpon that stone, vntill the time of Robert the First, king of Scotland." In another part of his "Historie of Scotland," Holinshed mentions king Simon Brech as having transmitted this stone to Ireland, about 700 years before the birth of Christ, and that "the first Fergus" brought it "out of Ireland into Albion," B.C. 330. One important property of this stone should not be unnoticed. It is said, by the writers from whom the foregoing particulars are derived, to furnish a test of legitimate royal descent; yielding an oracular sound when a prince of the true blood is placed upon it, and remaining silent under a mere pretender to the throne. We heard various joyful acclamations on the recent "royal day;" but (perhaps from that very circumstance) could not distinguish the sound in question.

Apart from these legends, the real history of the [Saxon: hagfail], or Fatal Stone [2], is curious; and has induced the learned Toland to call it "the antientest respected monument in the world [3]." It is to be traced, on the best authorities, into Ireland; whence it had been brought into Scotland, and had become of great notoriety in Argyleshire, some time before the reign of Kennith, or A.D. 834. This monarch found it at Dunstaffnage, a royal castle, enclosed it in a wooden chair, and removed it to the abbey of Scone, where for 450 years "all kingis of Scotland war crownit" upon it; or "quhil ye tyme of Robert Bruse. In quhais tyme, besyde mony othir crueltis done be kyng Edward Lang Schankis, the said chiar of merbyll wes taikin be Inglismen, and brocht out of Scone to London, and put into Westmonistar, quhaer it remains to our dayis [4]."

An ancient Irish prophecy, quoted by Mr. Taylor in his learned "Glory of Regality [5]," assures us, that the possession of this stone is essential to the preservation of regal power. It runs literally, "The race of Scots of the true blood, if this prophecy be not false, unless they possess the Stone of Fate, shall fail to obtain regal power." King Kennith caused the leonine verses following to be engraved on the chair:—

Ni fallat fatum
Scoti quocunque locatum
Invenient lapidem
Regnare tenentur ibidem.

Thus given by Camden,

Or Fate is blind,
Or Scots shall find,

> Where'er this stone
> A royal throne.

A prophecy which is said to have reconciled many a true Scot to the Union in Queen Anne's time; and which, since the extinction of the Stuart family, is remarkably fulfilled in the claims of the House of Brunswick,—George IV. being now the legitimate heir of both lines.

At or near a consecrated stone, it was an ancient Eastern custom to appoint kings or chieftains to their office. Thus we read in Scripture of Abimelech being "made king by the plain of the pillar that was in Shechem [6]," (the earliest royal appointment, perhaps, of which we have any traces in history;) and of Joash having the "crown put upon him" while he "stood by a pillar, as the manner was [7]." Subsequently, and among the northern nations, the practice "was to form a circle of large stones, commonly twelve in number, in the middle of which one was set up, much larger than the rest: this was the royal seat; and the nobles occupied those surrounding it, which served also as a barrier to keep off the people who stood without. Here the leading men of the kingdom delivered their suffrages, and placed the elected king on his seat of dignity [8]." From such places, afterwards, justice was frequently dispensed.

> "The old mun early rose, walk'd forth, and sate
> On polished stone, before his palace gate;
> With unguent smooth the lucid marble shone,
> Where ancient Neleus sate, a rustic throne."

Homer's *Odyss.* Pope's *Tr.* Γ. 496–10.

Thus arises the name of our Court of King's Bench.

At the coronation of our kings, the royal chair is now disguised in cloth of gold; but the wood-work, which forms its principal parts, is supposed to be the same in which Edward I. recased it, on bringing it to England.

Shakspeare's Richard III. inquires—

> "Is the *Chair* empty? Is the Sword unswayed?

Is the King dead? The empire unpossessed?
What heir of York is there alive but We?"

And the Earl of Richmond describes him, in admirable allusion to the foregoing facts, as

"A base foul *stone*, made precious by the foil
Of England's chair, where he is falsely set [9] ."

No. 2. *Of the Crowns.*

We, can only speak to the growth and antiquity of their present "fashion," none of those now used being of older date than the reign of Charles II. This monarch issued a commission for the "remakeing such royall ornaments and regalia" as the rebellious Parliament of his father had destroyed [10], in which "the old names and fashions" were directed to be carefully sought after and retained [11]. Upon this authority, we still have the national crown with which our monarchs are actually invested called St. Edward's, although the Great Seal of the Confessor exhibits him wearing a crown of a very different shape.

Whether the parent of our present crowns were the Eastern fillet, in the tying on which there was great ceremony, according to Selden,—the Roman or Grecian wreath, a "corruptible crown" of laurel, olive, or bay,—or the Jewish diadem of gold,—we shall leave to antiquarian research.

"This high imperial type of [England's] glory"

has slowly advanced, like the monarchy itself, to its present commanding size and brilliant appearance. From the coins and seals of the respective periods, several of our Anglo-Saxon princes appear to have worn only a fillet of pearl, and others a radiated diadem, with a crescent in front. Æthelstan's crown was of a more regular shape, resembling a modern earl's coronet. On king Alfred's there was the singular addition of "two little bells;" and the identical crown worn by this prince seems to have been long preserved at Westminster, if it were not the same which is described in the Parliamentary Inventory of 1642, as "King Alfred's crowne of gould wyer worke, sett with slight stones." Sir Henry Spelman thinks, there is some reason to conjecture that "the king fell upon the composing of an imperial crown;" but what could he mean by this accompaniment?

Gradually the crown grew from ear to ear, and then from the back to the forehead; sometimes it is represented as encircling a cap or helm, and sometimes without. William the Conqueror and his successor wore it on a cap adorned with points, and with "labels hanging at each ear [12];" the Plantagenets a diadem ornamented with fleurs de lis or strawberry leaves, between which were small globes raised, or points rather lower than the leaves; Richard III. or Henry VII. introduced the crosses; about the same time (on the coins of Henry VII.) the arches first appear; and the subsequent varieties of shape are in the elevation or depression of the arches. The maiden queen wore them remarkably high.

Blood's exploit with the new crown of Charles II. is told to all the young visitors at the Tower [13]. It is only wonderful that, in that age of plots, no political object or accusation was connected with it. The beautiful dialogue which our great dramatist puts into the mouth of Henry IV. and his son, who had taken the crown from his dying father's pillow, we could willingly transcribe entire: —

"*K. Henry.* O foolish youth!
Thou seek'st a greatness that will overwhelm thee.
Stay but a little; for my cloud of dignity
Is held from falling by so weak a wind,
That it will quickly drop; my day is dim.
Thou hast stolen that, which after some few hours
Were thine without offence; and at my death
Thou hast sealed up my expectation;
Thy life did manifest thou lovedst me not;
And thou wilt have me die assured of it.

"*P. Henry.* O pardon me, my Liege! but for my tears,
(The moist impediments unto my speech,)
I had forestalled this clear and deep rebuke,
Ere you with grief had spoke, and I had heard
The course of it so far. There is your crown —
And He that wears the crown immortally

> Long guard it yours! — —
> Coming to look on you, thinking you dead,
> (And dead almost, my Liege, to think you were,)
> I spake unto the crown, as having sense,
> And thus upbraided it. 'The care on thee depending
> Hath fed upon the body of my father;
> Therefore thou best of gold art worst of gold;
> Other, less fine in carat, is more precious,
> Preserving life, in medicine potable:
> But thou, most fine, most honoured, most renowned,
> Hast eat thy bearer up!'"

It is the same prince who afterwards so well apostrophizes his own greatness: —

> "O, be sick, great Greatness!
> And bid thy ceremony give thee cure.
> Think'st thou the fiery fever will go out
> With titles blown from adulation?
> Will it give place to flexure and low bending?
> Canst thou, when thou command'st the beggar's knee,
> Command the health of it? No, thou proud dream,
> That play'st so subtly with a king's repose,
> I am a king that find thee; and I know,
> 'Tis not the balm, the sceptre, and the ball,
> The sword, the mace, the crown imperial,
> The intertissued robe of gold and pearl,
> The farsed title running 'fore the king,
> The throne he sits on, nor the tide of pomp
> That beats upon the high shoar of this world;
> No, not all these thrice gorgeous ceremonies,
> Not all these, laid in bed majestical,
> Can sleep so soundly as the wretched slave."

No. 3. *The Sceptre*

Is a more ancient symbol of royalty than the crown. Homer speaks of "sceptred kings" — σκηπτουχοι βασιληεσ; and the book of Genesis, "of far elder memory," of a sceptre, as denoting a king or supreme governor [14]. There is a very early form of delivering this ensign of authority preserved in the Saxon coronation services; and the coins and seals of succeeding reigns usually place it in the hand of our monarchs. Very anciently, too, our kings received at their coronations a sceptre for the right hand, surmounted by a *cross*; and for the left, sometimes called the verge, one that terminated in a globe, surmounted by a *dove*. The two great symbols of the Christian religion are thus professedly embraced; but the monarch never appears with two sceptres except on this occasion.

No. 4. *The Ampulla, or Golden Eagle*

And the "holy oil" which is poured from it, are connected, like the royal chair, with some of the miracles that no one now believes, and with some interesting historical facts.

Amongst the honours bestowed by the Virgin on St. Thomas à Becket, (according to a MS. in the Cotton Library,) he received from our Lady's own hands, at Sens, in France, a golden eagle, and a small phial of stone or glass, containing an unction, on whose virtues she largely expatiated. Being then in banishment, he was directed to give them in charge to a monk of Poictiers, who hid them in St. Gregory's church at that place, where they were discovered in the reign of Edward III., with a written account of the vision; and, being delivered to the Black Prince, were deposited safely in the Tower. Henry IV. is said to be the first prince anointed with these vessels.

"Holy oil" still retains its use, if not its virtue, in our coronations. The king was formerly anointed on the head, the bowings of the arms, on both shoulders, and between the shoulders, on the breast, and on the hands; but the ceremonials of the last two coronations only prescribe the anointing of the head, breast, and hands. In these, too, nothing is said of the "consecration" of the oil, which seems anciently to have been performed on the morning of the coronation [15].

Historically, the custom of anointing kings is to be traced to the times of the Jewish judges; the consecration of one of whose descendants, Abimelech (before noticed), connects the subject with the earliest and one of the most beautiful fables of the East—

that of the trees going forth to anoint a king [16]. Selden regards this fable as a proof "that anointing of kings was of known use in the eldest times," and "that solemnly to declare one to be a king, and to anoint a king, in the Eastern parts, were but synonymies [17]." The elegant allusion to the olive tree, "honouring both God and man" with its "*fatness*" or oil, should not escape us, as corroborating this conjecture. This poem is dated by the learned antiquary "about 200 years before the beginning of the [Jewish] kingdom in Saul."

We have several instances in Scripture of the inauguration of the Jewish kings by anointing, and of its being performed at the express command of God [18]—a circumstance which was held to communicate an official sanctity to their persons, their attire, &c. The noble David twice spares the life of his bitterest enemy, Saul, upon this ground.—"Jehovah shall smite him," he says; "or his day shall come to die; or he shall descend into the battle, and perish"—"Who can stretch forth his hand against Jehovah's anointed, and be guiltless [19]?"—and he finely alludes to the general reverence of his country for these appointments, when he exclaims, in his memorable ode over his fallen rival, "The shield of the mighty is vilely cast away, the shield of Saul, as though it had not been anointed with oil!"

With the spread of Christianity, or rather of the papal domination, over the kingdoms of western Europe, came the adoption of this rite into the coronation ceremonies of its princes. It at once increased the influence of the church, and surrounded the monarch with a popular veneration. The three distinct anointings yet retained (*i.e.* on the head, breast, and hands or arms,) were said by Becket to indicate glory, holiness, and fortitude: another prelate, one of the greatest scholars of his age, assured our Henry III., that as all former sins were washed away in baptism, "so also by this unction [20]."

"Not all the water in the rough rude sea
Can wash the balm from an anointed king,"—

Richard II. is made to say, by Shakspeare, on the invasion of Bolingbroke. Sir Walter Scott, in his notes to Marmion, speaks of a singular ancient consecration of the kings of arms in Scotland, who seem to have had a regular coronation down to the middle of the sixteenth century,—only that they were anointed with *wine* instead of oil [21].

No. 5. *The Royal Swords*

Are named, *Curtana*, or the Sword of Mercy; the Sword of Justice to the Spirituality; the Sword of Justice to the Temporality; and the Sword of State. Of these the last alone is actually used in the coronation, being that with which the king is girded after his anointing; the rest are only carried before him by certain great officers. But Curtana has been honoured with a proper name since the reign of Henry III., at whose coronation it was carried by the Earl of Chester [22]. It is a flat sword, without a point; looking to which circumstance, and to its being also entitled the Sword of Mercy, some etymologists have traced it to the Latin *curto*, to cut short; while other writers, among whom is the learned Mr. Taylor, would transfer our researches to the scenes of ancient chivalry, and the exploits of Oger the Dane, or Orlando, as affording the title to this appendage of the monarchy, "The sword of Tristan," says this writer, "is found (ubi lapsus!) among the regalia of king John; and that of Charlemagne, *Joyeuse*, was preserved to grace the coronations of the kings of France. The adoption of these titles was, indeed, perfectly consonant with the taste and feeling of those ages, in which the gests of chivalry were the favourite theme of oral and historical celebration; and when the names of *Durlindana*, of *Curtein*, or *Escalibere*, would nerve the warrior's arm with a new and nobler energy [23]."

The Sword of Justice to the Spirituality is *obtuse*, that of Justice to the Temporality *sharp* at the point. "Henry VIII.," says a writer in a respectable periodical publication for July, "seems to have exercised his taste in endeavouring to abolish this discrepancy."

No. 6. *Of the Ring, Spurs, and Orb; and St. Edward's Staff.*

In the book of Genesis we read of Pharaoh's ring being given by him to Joseph, as a method of investing him with power: and thus the Persian monarch Ahasuerus transferred his authority to

Haman and to Mordecai [24]. What is added in the Scripture narration of one of these latter cases will illustrate the significancy of this mode of investiture. "Then were the king's scribes called, on the thirteenth day of the first month; and there was written according to all that Haman commanded unto the king's lieutenants, and to the governors that were over every province—to every people after their language; in the name of king Ahasuerus was it written, and *sealed* with the king's ring."

Of the golden ring with which our kings are invested, as "the ensign of royal dignity, and of defence of the catholic faith," there is yet another miracle of the coronation to relate. A certain "fayre old man" having asked alms of St. Edward the Confessor, he had nothing at hand to bestow upon him but his ring. Shortly after, two English pilgrims lost their way in the Holy Land, when "there came to them a fayr ancient man, wyth whyte heer for age. Thenne the olde man axed theym what they were, and of what regyon. And they answerde that they were pylgryms of England, and hadde lost theyr fellyshyp and way also. Thenne thys olde man comforted theym goodly, and brought theym in to a fayre cytee; and whanne they had well refreshed theym, and rested there alle nyhte, on the morne, this fayre olde man went with theym, and brought theym in the ryght waye agayne. And he was gladde to here theym talke of the welfare and holynesse of theyr kynge Saynt Edward. And whan he shold depart fro theym, thenne he tolde theym what he was, and sayd, 'I am Johan the Evangelyst; and saye ye vnto Edward your kyng, that I grete him well by the token that he gaff to me, thys *rynge*, with hys one handes [25].'"

By the exact mode that we have quoted from Scripture, do we find Offa, king of the East Angles, appointing Edmund as his successor; and with the ring, it is noticed, with which he had been invested at his own promotion to the royal dignity [26].

On the detention of James II. by the fishermen of Sheerness, in his first attempt at escape from this country, in 1688, it is particularly noticed in his Memoirs, "The king kept the diamond bodkin which he had of the queen's, and the *coronation ring*, which for more security he put into his drawers." The captain, it appeared, was well acquainted with the dispositions of his crew; (one of whom "cried out, 'It is father Petre—I know him by his lantern jaws;' a second called him an 'old hatchet-faced Jesuit;' and a third, 'a cunning old rogue, he would warrant him!') for, some time after he was gone, and probably by his order, several seamen entered the king's cabin, saying they must search him and the gentlemen, believing they had not given up all their money. The king and his companions told them that they were at liberty to do so, thinking that their readiness would induce them not to persist; but they were mistaken; the sailors began their search with a roughness and rudeness which proved they were accustomed to the employment: at last, one of them, feeling about the king's knee, got hold of the diamond bodkin, and cried out, with the usual oath, he had found a prize, but the king boldly declared he was mistaken. He had, indeed, scissors, a tooth-pick case, and little keys in his pocket, and what he felt was undoubtedly one of those articles. The man still seemed incredulous, and rudely thrust his hand into the king's pocket; but in his haste he lost hold of the diamond bodkin, and finding the things the king mentioned, remained satisfied it was so: by this means the bodkin and ring were preserved [27]." Whatever may be our opinion of the conduct of the monarch, we cannot follow him into these scenes without compassion for the *exile*, whose family seems to have been born to demonstrate how much of our pity unfortunate princes may claim, apart from their personal worth.

This is said to have been originally a favourite ring of the beautiful but unfortunate Mary queen of Scots; to have been sent by her, at her death, to James I.; through whom it came into the possession of our Charles I., and on *his* execution, was transmitted by bishop Juxon to his son. It lately came into the possession of his present Majesty, through the channels by which he has obtained all the remaining papers of the house of Stuart.

Richard II. resigned the crown to Henry IV. by transferring to him his ring. A paper was put into Richard's hands, from which he read an acknowledgment of being incapable of the royal office, and worthy, from his past conduct, to be deposed; that he freely absolved his subjects from their allegiance, and swore by the holy Gospels never to act in opposition to this surrender: adding, that if it were left wholly to him to name the future monarch, it should be Henry of Lancaster, to whom he then gave his ring [28].

The Spurs are a very ancient emblem of knighthood; in later coronations, the abundance of ceremonies has only allowed time for the king's heel to be touched with them. At the battle of Crecy, when Edward III. was requested to send reinforcements to his son, his reply was: "No; tell Warwick he shall have no assistance. Let the boy win his spurs [29]."

The Orb, or Mound (Fr. *monde*), is an emblem of sovereignty, said to be derived from imperial Rome; and to have been first adorned with the cross by Constantine, on his conversion to Christianity. It first appears among the royal insignia of England on the coins of Edward the Confessor; but Mr. Strutt authenticates a picture of Edgar, "made in the year 996," which represents that prince kneeling between two saints, who bear severally his sceptre and a globe surmounted by a cross [30]. This part of the regalia being inductive of supreme political power, has never been placed in the hands of any but kings or queens *regnant*. In the anomalous case of the coronation of William and Mary as joint sovereigns—the 'other world,' that Alexander wept for, was created; and the spare orb is still to be seen amongst the royal jewels of England!

The only remaining member of the regalia now in use is St. Edward's Staff; but whether so called from any of the pilgrimages of the Confessor—from its being designed to remind our monarchs of their being but pilgrims on earth—or simply from its being offered with the other regalia at that monarch's shrine, on the coronation of our kings, we have not the means of determining. All the regalia are supposed, indeed, to be in the custody of the Dean, as the successor of the Abbot of Westminster, at the period of each coronation.

No. 7. *The Royal Vestments*

Of England are amongst the most gorgeous "makings of a king" known to history. In the robes ordinarily designed to be worn in Parliament; and consisting of a surcoat of the richest crimson velvet, and a mantle and hood of the same, furred with ermine, and bordered with gold lace, the king first makes his appearance on the Coronation day; (on which he wears a *cap of state*, of the same materials, and at this time only.) These are, therefore, called his Parliament Robes, in distinction from the Robes of Estate, for which he exchanges them in the Abbey, at the close of the coronation, and which only differ from the former in being made of purple velvet.

These sumptuous external robes are of course laid aside during the anointing, and other parts of the coronation service.

The Armil, or Stole, is the only ecclesiastic symbol now retained in the investiture of our kings. In "MS. W. Y. in the College of Arms," quoted by Mr. Taylor, Henry VI. is said to have been "arrayed at the time of his coronation as a bishop that should sing mass, with a dalmatic like a tunic, and a stole about his neck [31]." This writer insists that the conductors of our English coronations since Henry VII.'s time (at the least) have very singularly mistaken the Stole for the Armil of more ancient times, and transferred to the latter the form of delivery originally designed for "a bracelet or royal ornament of the wrist." It is singular that the form in question should appear, as it certainly does, to suit either symbol. "Receive this armil as a token of the divine mercy embracing thee on every side [32]." The ornament at present in use embraces the neck.

§ 2. Anecdotes of the Disused Ceremonies of the Coronation.

We regard the coronation ceremonies of England as presenting a bird's-eye view of our history; and particularly of the various claims and privileges—and changes—of the monarchical branch of the Constitution. Some of these ceremonies, as we have seen, had their origin in those remote periods in which every believer in Revelation must accord "a divine right" to the kings of Judea; others are connected with the ancient hero-worship of our Pagan ancestors; while a third class perpetuate certain feudal rights and customs, of which they form the only distinct remaining traces. Some, again, are memorials of the triumph of our princes over the liberties of the people, while others present the plainest proof of the noble and successful struggles of the people against the encroachments of the crown.

The Recognition, with which the coronation, strictly so called, begins, is an elective rite, in which some of the more direct terms of appeal to the people are disused. Its title, "the Recognition," is of modern date [33]. After reciting the coronation oath, a respectable writer of queen Elizabeth's time thus gives the "sum of the English coronation." "Then doth the archbishop, turning about to the people, declare what the king *hath promised* and *sworn*, and by the mouth of an herald at arms asketh their *consents*, whether they be content to submit themselves unto this man as their king, or no, under the conditions proposed; whereunto when they have yielded themselves, then beginneth the archbishop to put upon him the regal ornaments [34]." Some of the questions anciently asked, accordingly, were, "Will you serve at this time, and give your good wills and assent to this same consecration, enunction, and coronation?"—To which the people answered, "Yea, yea." This was the form observed on the coronations of Edward VI., Henry VIII., and Henry VII. That of Henry VI.'s reign is curious. The archbishop made the "proclamacion on the iiij quarters of the scaffolde, seyend in this wyse: Sirs, heere comyth Henry, kyng Henryes sone the Vth, on whose sowle God have mercy, Amen. He humblyth hym to God and to holy cherche, askyng the crowne of this reame by right and defence of herytage; if ye hold ye pays with hym say Ya, and hold up handes. And then all the people cryed with oon voyce, Ye, ye [35]"

King John claimed the throne by "unanimous consent of the kingdom;" and the prelate of the day observed to the people that it was well known to them "that no man hath right of succession to this crown," except by such consent, and that "with invocation of the Holy Ghost, he be elected for his own deserts [36]."

During the Norman reigns it is evident that the coronation oath was administered before the recognition, and then the archbishop having stated what the king had engaged to do, asked the people if they would consent to take him for their king [37]? And of an earlier period, says Mr. Turner, "From the comparison of all the passages on this subject, the result seems to be that the king was elected at the Witenagemote, held on the demise of the preceding sovereign [38]."

On the whole, what is left of this ceremony seems rather unmeaning. The people are addressed, "ye that *are come* this day *to do* your homage, service, and bounden duty, are ye willing to do the same?" A feudal "recognition," and feudal "homage," it is not for the people, but the prelates and peers to perform; the ceremony, however, establishes what our history will corroborate, the undoubted right of the people to interfere with, and limit the succession of their princes, on extraordinary occasions, while it is the peaceful and sound policy of the Constitution to keep as near to the hereditary line as the emergency of the times shall allow.

It was at Edward VI.'s coronation that the ancient form of receiving the king's oath, prior to the recognition, was first reversed. — See the Chronological Anecdotes.

Coronations were anciently regarded as a species of parliamentary meeting between the king and his subjects. Writs of summons issued for the coronation of Edward II. are preserved in Rymer, which require the attendance of the people by their "knights, citizens, and burgesses;" and which differ very slightly from the ordinary parliamentary writs. Selden observes that at the coronation of Henry I. *clerus Angliæ et populus universus* were summoned to Westminster, "when divers lawes were both made and declared [39]."

The coronation oath has undergone some remarkable changes. The oath of Æthelred II. dated A.D. 978, is extant both in Latin and Anglo-Saxon, and agrees exactly with that of Henry I. preserved in the Cotton Library—a proof, as Lord Lyttleton observes, that even at the Conquest it was thought expedient to respect this fundamental compact between the prince and people. In the reign of Edward II. it first assumed the interrogatory form in which it is now administered, and remained in substance the same until the accession of Charles I. In this reign Archbishop Laud was accused of making both a serious interpolation, and an important omission in the coronation oath—a circumstance which, on his trial, brought its introductory clauses into warm discussion. Our forefathers had ever been jealous of all encroachments on what some copies of the old oath call "the lawes and customes of the people," by "old, rightfull, and devoute kings graunted;" and others "the laws, customs, and franchises granted to the clergy, and to the people by the glorious king St. Edward, according and conformable to the laws of God, the true profession of the Gospel established in this kingdom," &c. They had even compelled the Conqueror to engage repeatedly that these ancient statutes of the kingdom should not be violated; a stipulation renewed expressly in the great charter of his son Henry I. Laud was charged with adding, after the clause last quoted, the words "agreeable to the king's prerogative;" and of omitting these words, "which the people have chosen or shall choose." Of the latter charge he soon disposed by proving there were no such words in the oath of James I.; and on the former he remarks, "First, I humbly conceive this clause takes off none of the people's assurance. Secondly, that alteration, whatever it be, was not made by me—'tis not altogether improbable [it] was added in Edward VI. or Queen Elizabeth's time; and hath no relation at all to the laws of this kingdom *absolutely* mentioned before in the beginning of this oath; but only to the words, 'the profession of the Gospel established in this kingdom:' and then immediately follows 'and agreeing to the prerogative of the kings thereof,'—If this be the meaning, he that made the alteration, whoever it were, for I did it not, deserves thanks for it, and not the reward of a traitor [40]."

In James II.'s oath, as preserved by Sandford, and in which the precedent of Charles II.'s coronation was followed, we find both these alleged alterations!

On the accession of William and Mary it was enacted, that "as the [coronation] oath hath hitherto been framed in doubtful words and expressions, with relation to ancient laws and constitutions at this time unknown, and to the end that one uniform oath may be in all times to come taken by the kings and queens of this realm, and to them respectively administered at the time of their coronation," the oath, of which the following is a copy, should be taken by all succeeding sovereigns.

"*Abp.* Will you solemnly promise and swear to govern the people of this kingdom of England [now, this united kingdom of Great Britain and Ireland,] and the dominions thereunto belonging, according to the statutes in parliament agreed on, and the [respective [41]] laws and customs of the same?

King. I solemnly promise so to do.

Abp. Will you, to your power, cause law and justice, in mercy, to be executed in all your judgments?

King. I will.

Abp. Will you to the utmost of your power maintain the laws of God, the true profession of the Gospel, and the Protestant reformed Religion established by law? [Here was inserted, at the Union with Scotland, in 1707, And will you maintain and preserve inviolably the settlement of the Church of England, [now the united church of England and Ireland] and the doctrine, worship, discipline and government thereof as by law established, within the kingdoms of England and Ireland, the dominion of Wales and the town of Berwick-upon-Tweed, and the territories thereunto belonging, before the union of the two kingdoms [42]?] And will you preserve unto the bishops and clergy of England, and to the churches there committed to their charge, all such rights and privileges as by law do or shall appertain unto them or any of them?

King. All this I promise to do."

We have some slight traces in the history of our Anglo-Saxon kings of the Gothic mode of royal inauguration by the elevation of their princes. Eardnoulf, the second of those monarchs whose coronation is mentioned by our historians, was Ahoþen, lifted up to his royal seat, we are told by the Saxon Chronicle; and Athelstan received the royal unction at Kingston on a high scaffolding which exhibited him to the multitude [43]. This custom is no further worth noticing, than as a pagan rite which was soon disused, on the direction of these ceremonies being assumed by the church: and as being probably the origin of the existing mode of chairing members of parliament [44].

Anciently the king knelt while receiving the sacred unction from the prelate of the day, who sat in his chair at the high altar [45]: a deference to the priesthood which the kings of France retained to the period of the Revolution; and which the Roman Pontifical expressly requires. Since the Reformation our monarchs have also dispensed with "sprinkling the crown with holy water" and "censing it" before it is made use of in these important ceremonies—duties of the archbishop which are laid down in the Liber Regalis, of the dean and chapter of Westminster.

There seems to have been a double anointing of our kings at their respective coronations until the reign of James I. or Charles I.; that is, after the present use of the unction on the hands, breast, &c.; the *chrism* of the Catholic church was applied, in formâ crucis, on the forehead. The distinct signification of this anointing we cannot discover, even after a late learned attempt to elucidate it [46]. The sign of the cross, a symbolical acknowledgment of the Christian faith used in the anointing, we retain: but the *two* vessels, the eagle and vial of the ancient ceremonies (so intelligently provided by the Virgin; see our last section) establish the fact of a double anointing having at one time obtained.

But the most important ceremonies of the coronation which the superior economy, or superior intelligence, of modern times has taught us to omit, are the special creation of Knights of the Bath on this occasion, and the progress of the court from the Tower, through London.

The ancient and noble order in question was so far very appropriately connected with the assumption of a sovereignty partly feudal, as it formed one of the most splendid feudal distinctions. It was conferred with great solemnity, among the Franks and Saxons, long prior to the Conquest; at which period our first William is shown by Mr. Anstey, to have been in the habit of bestowing it both in his Norman and English dominions. The candidate for that honour was required to keep his vigils with great strictness, after a previous ablution from which the name of the order is derived, and which were together meant to indicate the moral purity required of him; as the motto "*Tria juncta in uno*" implied a peculiar devotion to the honour of the Holy Trinity.

The coronation of Henry IV. however, first brings it prominently into notice in our history. That prince, having compelled the unfortunate Richard II.

> "With his own tears to wash away his balm,
> With his own hands to give away the crown,
> With his own tongue deny his sacred state;"

was anxious to give those "sun-shine days" to the people which should induce them to forget the stormy commencement of his reign. Froissart describes him as proceeding with great pomp from Westminster to the Tower, "on the Saturday before his coronation." This was at that time "the castle royall and cheefe howse of safetye in this kingdome." Hither, therefore, many of our princes repaired for security until "all things of royal apparell and pompe necessarye and proper" to the coronation could be arranged. "Those squires who were to be knighted watched their arms that night: they amounted to forty-six; each squire had his chamber and bath, in which he bathed. The ensuing day the duke of Lancaster (Henry IV.) after mass, created them knights, and presented them with long green coats, with straight sleeves lined with minever, after the manner of prelates. These knights had on their left shoulders a double cord of white silk, with white tufts hanging down."

Henry VI. created thirty-six knights on his coronation; Edward IV. thirty-two; and Charles II. sixty-eight. The marriages of the royal family, the birth of heirs to the crown, and the fitting out of military expeditions of importance, furnish other accessions to the order during this long period. After the reign of Charles II. this part of the ceremonial was omitted; and the order, in fact, discontinued until the accession of the House of Brunswick [47].

The princes of this august house, however, have not revived the custom of an extraordinary creation of knights as a part of the coronation ceremonies.

The other ancient and disused custom of a royal progress from the Tower to Westminster is a theme of admiration with several of our old chroniclers, and must have been a highly interesting and popular accompaniment of the royal pageant.

The monarch, ordinarily, dined at the Tower on the day after the creation of the Knights of the Bath; and devoted the greater part of the day, *after* dinner, to this prolonged exhibition of himself to the people. Charles II. dined at what is called an "early" hour, in the "account" of sir Edward Walker, i.e. nine o'clock in the morning, on this occasion.

Froissart thus gives us the progress of Henry IV. "The duke of Lancaster left the Tower this Sunday after dinner, on his return to Westminster: he was bare-headed, and had round his neck the order of the king of France. The prince of Wales, six dukes, six earls, eighteen barons, accompanied him; and there were, of knights and other nobility, from eight to nine hundred horse with the procession. The duke was dressed in a jacket of the German fashion, of cloth of gold, mounted on a white courser, with a blue garter on his left leg. He passed through the streets of London, which were all handsomely decorated with tapestries and other rich hangings: there were nine fountains in Cheapside, and other streets he passed through, which perpetually ran with white and red wines. He was escorted by prodigious numbers of gentlemen, with their servants in liveries and badges; and the different companies of London were led by their wardens, clothed in their proper livery, and with ensigns of their trade. The whole cavalcade amounted to six thousand horse, which escorted the duke from the Tower to Westminster [48]."

Or, as Shakspeare brings every movement of a similar procession of this monarch before us,

"Mounted upon a hot and fiery steed,
Which his aspiring rider seemed to know,
With slow but stately pace, kept on his course:
While all tongues cried, God save thee, Bolingbroke!
You would have thought the very windows spake,
So many greedy looks of young and old
Through casements darted their desiring eyes
Upon his visage; and that all the walls
With painted imagery had said at once
Jesu preserve thee! welcome Bolingbroke!
Whilst he, from one side to the other turning,
Bare-headed, lower than his proud steed's neck,
Bespoke them thus; I thank you, countrymen;
And thus still doing, thus he past along [49]."

The coronation of Elizabeth the queen of Henry VII. includes one of the most splendid royal progresses on record. It will be recollected by our readers that this prince exhibited a strong personal reluctance to marry Elizabeth as well as to her subsequent coronation; although his union with her extinguished the bloody feuds of the houses of York and Lancaster, and bequeathed to posterity the invaluable boon of an undisputed succession to the throne. The Commons, in presenting him on his accession with the usual grant of tonnage and poundage, took the liberty to add their desire that he would "take to wife and consort the Princess Elizabeth, which marriage they hoped God would bless with a progeny of the race of kings," (*de stirpe regum* [50], the united race, perhaps, is meant). But it was not until a pretender to the throne had shaken the regal authority to its base, that, eighteen months after his marriage, he prepared for the coronation of his queen. A very superior modern historian [51] thus expresses the feelings of the prince and people on this occasion: —

"From this insurrection [that which was terminated by the battle of Stoke] the king learned an important lesson, that it was not his interest to wound the feelings of those whose principles had attached them to the house of York. His behaviour to the queen had created great discontent. Why, it was asked, was she not crowned? Why was she, the rightful heir to the crown, refused the usual honours of royalty? Other kings had been eager to crown their consorts: but Elizabeth had now been married a year and a half; she had borne the king a son to succeed to the throne; and yet she was kept in obscurity, as if she were unworthy her station."

The orders which he now gave, therefore, for her public investiture with the royal dignity, were calculated fully to conciliate the popular feeling. On the Friday preceding her coronation fourteen gentlemen were created knights of the Bath, and on the same day "the queene's good grace, royally apparelled, and accompanyed with my ladie the king's mother, and many other great estates, bothe lordes and ladies, richely besene, came forward to the coronacion; and, at their coming furth from Grenewich by water, there was attending upon her there, the maior, shrifes, and aldermen of the citie, and divers and many worshipfull comoners, chosen out of every craft, in their levereyes, in barges freshly furnished with banners and stremers of silke, richely beaton with the armes and bagges of their craftes; and, in especially, a barge called the bachelor's barge, garnished and apparelled passing all other; wherein was ordeynid a great redde dragon spowting flames of fyer into the Thamess, and many other gentlemanlie pagiaunts, well and curiously devised to do her highness sporte and pleasure with. And her grace, thus royally apparelled and accompanied, and also furnished in every behalf with trumpettes, claryons, and other mynstrelleys as apperteynid and was fitting to her estate roial, came from Grenewich aforesaid, and landed at the Toure wharfe, and enterid into the Toure; where the king's highnes welcomed her in such maner and fourme as was to all the estates and others there being present, a very good sight, and right joyous and comfortable to beholde [52]."

Next day she went in procession from the Tower to Westminster, dressed in white cloth of gold of damask, with a mantle of the same furred with ermine. Reclining on a litter, she wore

"Her faire yelow haire hanging downe plaine behynd her bak, with a calle of pipes over it;" and confined only on the forehead by a circlet of gold, ornamented with precious stones. An elegant canopy of cloth of gold was borne over her by four knights of the body; and immediately behind her rode four baronesses on grey palfreys. The streets on this occasion were "clensed, dressed, and beseene with clothes of tapestrie and arras; and some, as Cheepe, hanged with rich clothe of golde, velvet, and silke; and along the streets, from the Toure to Powles, stode in order all the craftes of London in their liveries; and in divers places of the citie were ordeynid singing children, some arayed like angelles, and other like virgins, to sing swete songes as her grace passed by [53]."

Similar accounts are given by Hall of the progress of Henry VIII. and Catherine of Arragon through the city. "The streates were railed and barred on the one side; from over ageynst Grace churche unto Bredstreate in Chepeside, where every occupacion stode in their liveries in ordre, beginnyng with base and meane occupacions, and so ascendyng to the worshipfull craftes; highest and lastly stode the maior with the aldermen. The goldsmithes stalles, unto the ende of the Olde Chaunge, beeing replenished with virgins in white, with braunches of white waxe; the priestes and clerkes in rich copes with crosses and censers of silver, censying his grace and the quene also as they passed [54]." The latter was borne on a litter by two white palfreys, trapped in cloth of gold.

Anne Boleyn's progress must not be unnoticed. Like Elizabeth's, it began with a voyage from Greenwich, and the creation of a due number of knights "bathed and shryven according to the old vsuage of England."—"The high stretes where the queene should passe were all graveled from the Toure to Temple barre, and railed on the one side; within whiche rayle stode the craftes along in their order. And before the quene and her traine should come, Cornehill and Gracious Street were hanged with fyne scarlet, crimson and other greyned clothes, and in some place with rich arras, tapestry, and carpettes, and the moste part of the Chepe was hanged with clothe of tyssue, golde, velvet, and many riche hangings whyche made a goodlie shewe."

Her connexion with the French court, it is to be supposed, suggested the appearance of "xii Frenchmen, whiche were belongyng to the Frenche ambassador," coming "fyrst" in her "company—in coats of blewe velvet, with sleves of yelowe and blewe velvet, and their horses trapped with close trappers of blewe sarcenet, powdered with white crosses." The French ambassador also rode before her.

At Gracious Church street was a costly and a marveilous connyng pageaunt, made by the merchauntes of the Styllarde, for there was the Mount Penasus, with the fountayne of Helycon, which was of white marble, and iiii streames, without pype, did rise an elle hye and mette together in a litle cuppe above the fountain, which ranne abundantly Racke and Rennishe wyne 'til night! On the mountaine satte Apollo, and at his feete satte Calliope, and on every side of the mountaine satte iiii Muses playing on several swete instrumentes, and at their feete Epigrammes and Poyses were written in golden letters, with the which every Muse, accordyng to her propertie, praised the Quene.—"At the conduite in Cornhill there were thre graces set in a throne; afore whom was the *spryng of grace* continually ronnyng—wine!" At the cross in Chepe, "Master Baker, the recorder, with lowe reverence, makyng a proper and briefe proposicion—gave to her, in the name of the citie, 1000 marks of golde in a purse of golde [55]." This was the last time (we mean no reflection on its inhabitants,) that the Muses and Graces exhibited themselves on such an occasion in the city. Hereafter the zeal of contending religious parties in the state taught them to choose other emblems of their desires and anticipations.

Edward VI.'s progress exhibited Valentine and Orson, "in Cheap," at due distance from whom stood Sapience and the Seven Liberal Sciences, who "declared certaine goodly speeches," for the instruction of the young king. Various other allegorical personages harangued him by the way; but the most singular spectacle was that whereby "Paul's steple laie at anchor," as Holinshed expresses it. An Arragosen made fast a rope to the battlements of St. Paul's, which was also attached to an anchor at the gate of the dean's house; and descended upon it in the sight of the king and assembled populace, to the no small gratification of both.

His sister Mary was welcomed into the city by "one Peter, a Dutchman," who placed himself on the weathercock of St. Paul's, holding "a streamer in his hand five yards long;" occasionally kneeling down on the said weathercock, "to the great marvell of the people," and balancing himself sometimes on one foot and sometimes on another.

In her procession appeared "the ladie Elizabeth and the ladie Anne of Cleve;" the queen rode in a chariot of cloth of tissue, her sister following in "another chariot having a covering of cloth of silver."—"She sat in a gowne of purple velvet, furred with powdered ermins, having on her head a kall of cloth of tinsell, béeset with pearle and stone, and above the same, vppon her head, a round circlet of gold, béeset so richlie with pretius stones, that the value thereof was inestimable; the same kall and circle being so massie and ponderous, that she was faine to beare vp her head with her hand."

Holinshed is very garrulous on the progress of the Virgin Queen, although he singularly enough omits all details of the principal parts of her coronation.

"On Thursdaie the twelfe of Januari (1559), the queene's maiestie remooved from her palace at Westminster, by water, vnto the tower of London, the lord mayor and aldermen in their barge, and all the citizens with their barges decked and trimmed with targets and banners of their mysteries accordinglie, attending on her grace. The bachellers barge of the lord maior's companie, to wit, the mercers', had their barge with a foist trimmed with three tops, and artillerie aboord, gallantlie appointed to wait vpon them, shooting off lustilie as they went, with great and pleasant melodie of instruments, which plaied in most swete and heavenlie maner. Her grace shut (shot) the bridge about two of the clocke in the after noone, at the still of the ebbe, the lord maior and the rest following after her barge, attending the same, till her maiestie tooke lande at the privie staires at the tower wharfe."

"At her entring the citie" a variety of pageants were prepared to express the "praiers, wishes, and welcommings" of her loving people, which we cannot attempt to particularize. "If a man should saie well," remarks our chronicler, "he could not better terme the citie of London that time than a stage wherein was shewed the woonderfull spectacle of a noble hearted princesse toward her most loving people, and the people's exceeding comfort in beholding so woorthie a soveraigne, and hearing so princelike a voice."

The Muses had, indeed, quitted "the citie"—and miserable enough are the ditties which Holinshed gives us from the mouth of the various children "who expounded the pageants:" some appropriate devices were, however, mixed up with much child's-play. The union of the red and white roses on the marriage of Henry VII. (the queen's grandfather) with Elizabeth of York, was commemorated by personages representing the king and queen, sitting with hands joined together by the ring of matrimony; "and all emptie places of this pageant were furnished with sentences concerning vnitie."—"This pageant was grounded upon the queen's name," adds our historian, "For like as the long warre betweene the two houses of Yorke and Lancaster then ended, when Elizabeth, daughter to Edward the Fourth, matched in marriage with Henrie the Seventh, heire to the house of Lancaster: so—the queene maiestie's name was Elizabeth, and for so much as she is the onlie heir of Henrie the Eighth, which came of both houses, [she was] the knitting vp of concord." The eight beatitudes expressed in the fifth chapter of the gospell of Saint Matthew "applied to our soveraigne ladie Elizabeth," were at "Soper Lane end," in Chepe: but the pageant presenting an English Bible to the queen was particularly well devised. Our readers will take the poetry as by far the best specimen of the productions of the day. Between two hills, representing a flourishing and a decayed commonwealth, "was made artificiallie one hollow place or cave, with doore and locke inclosed, out of the which, a little before the queenes' highnesse commyng thither, issued one personage, whose name was Time, apparalled as an old man, with a sieth in his hand, havinge winges artificiallie made, leading a personage of lesser stature than himselfe, which was finelie and well apparalled, all clad in white silke, and directly over her head was set her name and title in Latin and English, Temporis filia, the daughter of Time. Which two, as appointed, went forwards toward the south side of the pageants, and on her brest was written her proper name, which was Veritas, Truth, who held a book in her hand, upon the which was written Verbum Veritas, the Word of Truth. And out of the south side of the pageant was cast a standing for a child, which should interpret the same pageant. Against whom when the queen's maiestie came, he spake vnto her grace these sweet words:—

> "This old man with a sieth
> Old father Time they call,
> And her his daughter Truth,
> Which holdeth yonder booke:
> Whome he out of his nooke
> Hath brought foorth to us all,
> From whence this manie yeares
> She durst not once out looke.
>
> "Now sith that Time againe
> His daughter Truth hath brought,
> We trust, ô worthie queene,
> Thou wilt this truth embrace,
> And sith thou vnderstandst
> The good estate and naught,
> We trust wealth thou wilt plant,
> And barrenesse displace.
>
> "But for to heale the sore
> And cure that is not seene;
> Which thing the booke of truth,
> Dooth teach in writing plaine:
> Shee doth present to thee
> The same, ô worthie queene,
> For that, that words doo flie,
> But written dooth remaine."

"Thus the queene's highnesse passed through the citie, which, without anie foreigne person, of itself beautified itselfe, and received her grace at all places, as hath been before mentioned, with most tender obedience and love, due to so gratious a queene and sovereigne a ladie."

James I. made the most important "progress" for himself and family that we have yet recorded; when, as tranquilly as ever the crown of England had descended from father to son, the house of Stuart succeeded that of Tudor on the throne of Great Britain. Nor was his journey from Edinburgh to London unobserved by the people. They are said to have contrasted his hauteur and reserve at this period with the well-remembered affability and popular manner of Elizabeth on such occasions; but neither does his coronation progress, nor that of his immediate successors, Charles I. or II. (with whom this usage terminated) present any new features of interest. The great object of the conductors of the ceremony was to conform to the ancient precedents; while the personal disposition of each of the sovereigns of this house was to retain as much of the demi-god as possible in these stately movements of the monarch.

§ 3. Anecdotes of the Assistant Offices of the Coronation.

The assistant offices of the coronation are, for the far greater part, ecclesiastical or hereditary. They are connected therefore with all the religious changes, and family honours of the empire. The nobility bear in person a part in the royal day, and approach and actually touch that crown, from which, as the fountain of honour, they seem to renew, and re-invigorate, their most ancient claims to distinction: while the metropolitan of the English Church enjoys the exclusive right of consecrating and crowning the monarch.

As early as the Norman Conquest, this privilege of the see of Canterbury is spoken of as well-established; and but two subsequent instances occur of its being overlooked or denied: both remarkably associated with the history of the papal power in this country [56]. In the first, that of the coronation by the archbishop of York of prince Henry, son of Henry II., may be traced the incipient cause of the assassination of archbishop Becket, whose martyrdom became conducive to the highest triumphs of that power: in the second, queen Elizabeth's coronation by Oglethorpe, bishop of Carlisle, and the refusal of all the other prelates to assist in the ceremony, we behold its dying struggles for a dominion never more to be renewed.

Mr. Lingard, who, as a Catholic, may be supposed to state these transactions with a sufficient leaning to his own church, as expressly connects the murder of Becket with a jealousy on this subject as any other of our historians. Henry II. had employed the known enemy of the archbishop, Roger of York, in the consecration of his son above alluded to; but the primate and the king met on friendly terms at Rouen, in the following month; they compromised their differences; and the former set out on his return to his diocese. The Pope, however, "before he heard of the reconciliation, had issued letters of suspension or excommunication against the bishops who had officiated at the late coronation." The archbishop had at one time resolved to suppress these letters, our historian admits; and surely it was now an imperative duty so to do. But the prelates concerned, it seems, who knew that he carried them about him, had assembled at Canterbury, and sent to the coast Ranulf de Broc, with a party of soldiers, to search him on his landing, and take them from him. Information of the design reached him at Witsand: and "in a moment of irritation," says Mr. L., "he despatched them before himself by a trusty messenger, by whom, or by whose means, they were publicly delivered to the bishops in the presence of their attendants. It was a precipitate and unfortunate measure, the occasion, at least, of the catastrophe that followed."

The prelates hastened to Normandy to demand redress and protection from the king; who, irritated by their representation, exclaimed: "Of the cowards who eat my bread, is there not one, who will free me from this turbulent priest?" and the blood of Becket flowed a few days after in reply. When he asked one of his assassins, "What is thy object?" he was told that he must instantly absolve the bishops—"Till they offer satisfaction, I will not," said the primate. "Then die," exclaimed his murderers, and closed around him [57].

The *Lord Great Chamberlain's* office commences with carrying the king his shirt on the morning of the coronation, and assisting the chamberlain of the household to dress his majesty. Queens regnant depute this office to some of the ladies of the household: we are told that the celebrated duchess of Marlborough last enjoyed it, at the coronation of queen Anne.

The office gives a claim to all the furniture of the royal chamber, in which its duties begin. The idea of our ancestors was, that the coronation, and particularly the consecration of a king, conferred new honours and talents of the most sacred and extraordinary description. He was now made a new man, and elevated into a new order of beings;

> "Consideration, like an angel, came
> And whipt the offending Adam out of him;
> Leaving his body as a paradise,
> To envelope and contain celestial spirits [58]."

Hence every part of his office was new and kingly. Froissart describes the consecration of Henry IV. immediately after the recognition, thus: "after this the duke descended from his throne, and advanced to the altar to be consecrated. This ceremony was performed by two archbishops and ten bishops: he was stripped of all his royal state before the altar, naked to his shirt, and was then anointed and consecrated in six places; that is to say, on the head, the breast, the shoulders, before and behind, on the back and hands: they then placed a bonnet on his head; and while this was doing, the clergy chaunted the litany, a service that is performed to hallow a font [59]." The lord chamberlain is official governor of the palace for the time being, and the principal personal attendant of the king.

The *Lord High Constable* also attends the royal person, assists at the reception of the regalia from the dean and chapter of Westminster, and, together with the earl Marshal, ushers the champion into the hall.

Of the Royal Championship.

Whether we consider its uninterrupted exercise, and that by one family, for so many centuries, its feudal import, or its present splendid and imposing effect, the office of champion certainly eclipses all the other services of the coronation.

Since the coronation of Richard II. A.D. 1377, (of which there is in Walsingham a detailed account) this office has been performed by a Dymoke, the head of the family of that name who have held the manor of Scrivelsby in Lincolnshire, worth about £1200 per annum, by the tenure of this service. During the reigns of Edward II. and III. the right was in dispute: prior to that period and from the days of the Conqueror it was vested in the far-famed family of Marmion, whose chief, as

> "— — Lord of Fontenay,
> Of Lutterworth and Scrivilbaye,
> Of Tamworth tower and town,"

came from Normandy with William, and is there supposed to have held the first of these possessions, on condition of performing the service of champion to the successive dukes.

At the conquest the feudal system was established in England in its maturest and strictest forms; and the present office being the most perfect relic of that system known to modern times, a slight sketch of its peculiarities will not be uninteresting.

The foundation of all the subsequent customs of homage, suit, service, purveyance, &c. is to be traced in the original connexion between the vassal and his lord, or the chief and his retainers, which Tacitus notices as remarkable in ancient Germany. According to this, every follower was to be found fighting by the side of his chief in time of war, as the very first duty of social life — and in time of peace to look up to him as the only legitimate fountain of honour and justice.

Certain it is, that this relation was, in substance, as well known and supported by our Anglo-Saxon ancestors, before the accession of William, as it was by our Highland neighbours, down to the rebellion in 1745. A striking instance of the romantic and desperate courage to which it gave rise occurs as early as the reign of Cynewulf, king of Wessex, A.D. 784. Sigebircht, the deposed predecessor of this prince, was, in the first year of his rival's reign, found murdered in the forest of Andreswald: but left a brother, of the name of Cyneheard, who cherished for thirty-one years the secret purpose of avenging his death. At last he returned, with eighty-four retainers, into the neighbourhood of Winchester, the royal residence; and, tracing the king to a country seat at Merton, the abode of a favourite lady, surrounded the house at midnight. Cynewulf was quickly roused; but his followers were scattered throughout the place, and could not be collected until, after a brave personal conflict with the enemy, the king's life-blood had satiated his vengeance. Cyneheard now offered the royal train their liberty and possessions, on condition of their peaceable departure; but they rejected his proposals with scorn, and to a man died on the threshold of their master. On the intelligence reaching the court, in the morning, Osric and Wavirth, two powerful chieftains, surrounded themselves with their vassals, and rode to Merton, where they were met by Cyneheard, with professions of friendship. He called their attention to the injuries of his family, the duty of avenging which had devolved upon himself; urged his claim to the vacant throne; made them the most liberal offers, in case of their acknowledgment of him; and concluded by reminding them, that many of his adherents were their own near kinsmen. "Our kinsmen," they indignantly answered, "are not dearer to us than was our lord. To his murderer we shall never submit. If those who are related to us wish to save their lives, let them depart." "The same offer," rejoined the followers of Cyneheard, "was made to the attendants of the king, who refused it. We will prove to-day that our attachment is equal to theirs:" and Cyneheard, and all his adherents except one, were slain [60].

But the Conqueror, owing his crown to the sword, more strictly adapted the system which he found in use to his own military notions and future safety. Having divided all the principal estates of the country amongst his vassals, he converted the English military tenures into a regular obligation, called knights' fees, which compelled each tenant in chief to have a certain number of knights, or horsemen, always ready to assert the rights of the crown, and to fight under its banner, in any cause, "We will," says a law on this subject, yet extant, "that *all* the freemen of our kingdom possess their lands in peace, free of all tollage and unjust exaction: that nothing be required or taken from them but their free service, which they owe to us of right, as has been appointed to them, and granted by us with hereditary right for ever, by the common council of our whole kingdom." "And we command that all earls, barons, knights, serjeants, and freemen, be always provided with horses and arms as they ought; and that they be always ready to perform to us their whole service, in manner as they owe it to us of right, for their fees and tenements, and as we have appointed to them by the common council of our whole kingdom, and as we have granted to them in fee a right of inheritance [61]." This free service required the due quota of horsemen, which each vassal was to furnish, to come, completely armed, on his requisition, and to be maintained under the royal command, at the charge of the party sending them, for forty days. Even the dignitaries of the church, and monastic bodies holding lands, were not exempt from this service.

Each tenant in chief subdivided his property into subvassalships, imposing a similar service, and carrying downwards all the obligations of homage, fealty, and personal attendance on all important occasions.

Out of such a system, that a favoured vassal should be selected to assert the personal right of the monarch to his throne, will appear very natural: it is only surprising that the violence and constant habit of appealing to the sword, in which this with the other feudal claims originated, should have left it to flow on in such an uninterrupted course — a course of succession far more regular than the transmission of the crown it is supposed to defend.

The championship is connected also with a remarkable feature of ancient jurisprudence, the wager of battle, recently abolished. This was regarded as an appeal to the judgment of *God*; and succeeded, at the Conquest, the fires and other ordeals of our ancestors, which the Normans affected to despise. The reader, however, may be disposed to conjecture, that as much of the divine interposition might be expected to decide the healing of a burn or scald, as the issue of a battle. The older custom was for the accused to plunge his hand into a cauldron of boiling water, and take out a stone or piece of iron of a given weight; the depth of the vessel being proportionate to the magnitude of the crime charged: or for him to seize, at the end of a religious service, a bar of iron placed on a fire at the beginning of the service, and run over a certain length of ground with it: the method in which the wounds healed, in either case, being the criterion of guilt or innocence.

The wager of battle was certainly of more splendid pretensions, and was introduced at first with these stipulations. If the opposite parties were countrymen, they were to follow their national customs, whatever they were; if the appellee were a foreigner, or of foreign descent, he might offer wager of battle, and on its being declined, purge himself by his own oath and that of his witnesses, according to the Norman law; or if a native of the country, he might have his choice of the trial by ordeal or by battle.

The solemn feelings and great religious sincerity with which our forefathers regarded combats of this description, cannot be more powerfully or more accurately depicted, than in the memorable combat scene of Ivanhoe: —

"The draw-bridge fell, the gates opened, and a knight, bearing the great standard of the order, sallied from the castle, preceded by six trumpets, and followed by the knights preceptors, two and two, the grand master coming last, mounted on a stately horse, whose furniture was of the simplest kind. Behind him came Brian de Bois Guilbert, armed cap-a-pee in bright armour, but without his lance, shield, or sword, which were borne by his two esquires behind him. — He looked ghastly pale, as if he had not slept for several nights, yet reined in his pawing war-horse with the habitual ease and grace proper to the best lance of the Order of the Temple. His general appearance was grand and commanding; but looking at him with attention, men read that in his dark features from which we willingly withdraw our eyes.

"On either side rode Conrade of Mont Fitchet and Albert de Malvoisin, who acted as godfathers to the champion. They were in their robes of peace, the white dress of the order. Behind them followed other knights companions of the Temple, with a long train of esquires and pages, clad in black, aspirants to the honour of being one day knights of the order."

After these walked the accused in a coarse white dress, surrounded by wardens in sable livery.

"The slow procession moved up the gentle eminence, on the summit of which was the tilt-yard, and entering the lists, marched once around them from right to left, and when they had completed the circle made a halt. There was then a momentary bustle while the grand-master and his attendants" took their places: when "a long and loud flourish of trumpets announced that the court was seated for judgment. Malvoisin, then acting as godfather to the champion, stepped forward and laid the glove of the Jewess, which was the pledge of battle, at the feet of the grand-master.

"Valourous lord and reverend father," said he, "here standeth the good knight Brian de Bois Guilbert, knight preceptor of the Order of the Temple, who by accepting the pledge of battle which I now lay at your reverence's feet, hath become bound to do his devoir in combat this day, to maintain that this Jewish maiden, by name Rebecca, hath justly deserved the doom passed upon her—condemning her to die as a sorceress. Here, I say, he standeth such battle to do knightly and honourably, if such should be your noble and sanctified pleasure."

"Hath he made oath," said the grand-master, "that his quarrel is just and honourable? Bring forward the crucifix and the *Te igitur*."

"Sir and most reverend father," answered Malvoisin readily, "our brother here present hath already sworn to the truth of his accusation, in the hand of the good knight Conrade de Mont Fitchet, and otherwise he ought not to be sworn, seeing his adversary is an unbeliever and may take no oath."

"The grand-master having allowed the apology, commanded the herald to stand forth and do his devoir. The trumpets then flourished, and a herald stepping forward, proclaimed aloud, "Oyez, oyez, oyez. Here standeth the good knight Sir Brian de Bois Guilbert, ready to do battle with any knight of free blood who will sustain the quarrel allowed and allotted to the Jewess Rebecca, to try by champion in respect of lawful essoigne of her own body; and to such champion the reverend and valorous grand-master here present allows a fair field, an equal partition of sun and wind, and whatever else appertains to a fair combat." The trumpets again sounded, and there was a dead pause of many minutes.—

"The judges had now been two hours in the lists, awaiting in vain the appearance of a champion.

"It was the general belief, that no one could or would appear for a Jewess accused of sorcery, and the knights, instigated by Malvoisin, whispered to each other, that it was time to declare the pledge of Rebecca forfeited. At this instant a knight, urging his horse to speed, appeared on the plain, advancing towards the lists. An hundred voices exclaimed, 'A champion,' 'a champion!'

And, despite the prepossession and prejudices of the multitude, they shouted unanimously as the knight rode into the tilt-yard. The second glance, however, served to destroy the hope that his timely arrival had excited. His horse, urged for many miles to its utmost speed, appeared to reel from fatigue, and the rider, however undauntedly he presented himself to the lists, either from weakness, weariness, or both, seemed scarce able to support himself in the saddle.

"To the summons of the herald who demanded his rank, his name and purpose, the strange knight answered readily and boldly, 'I am a good knight and noble, come hither to sustain with lance and sword the just and lawful quarrel of this damsel, Rebecca, daughter of Isaac of York; to uphold the doom pronounced against her to be false, and truthless, and to defy Sir Brian de Bois Guilbert as a traitor, murtherer, and liar; as I will prove in this field with my body against his, by the aid of God, our Lady, and of Monseigneur Saint George, the good knight.'

"The stranger must first show," said Malvoisin, "that he is a good knight, and of honourable lineage. The Temple sendeth not forth her champion against nameless men."

"My name," said the knight, raising his helmet, "is better known, my lineage more pure, Malvoisin, than thine own. I am Wilfrid of Ivanhoe." — "Rebecca", said he, riding up to the fatal chair, "dost thou accept of me for thy champion?"

"I do," she said, "I do!" fluttered by an emotion which the fear of death was unable to produce.

— "Ivanhoe was already at his post, and had closed his visor, and assumed his lance. Bois Guilbert did the same.

— "The herald then, seeing each champion in his place, uplifted his voice, repeating thrice, *Faites vos devoirs, preux chevaliers*. After the third cry, he withdrew to one side of the lists, and again proclaimed, that none on peril of instant death should dare by word, cry, or action, to interfere with, or disturb this fair field of combat. The grand-master, who held in his hand the gage of battle, Rebecca's glove, now threw it into the lists, and pronounced the fatal signal words, *Laissez aller*. The trumpets sounded, and the knights charged each other in full career."

The result arising out of the peculiar situation of one of the combatants toward Rebecca, was his almost immediate death: but, seeing him fall, Wilfrid assumed the rights of a victor, and "placing his foot on his breast, and the sword point to his throat, commanded him to yield or die on the spot. Bois Guilbert returned no answer.

"Slay him not, sir knight," said the grand-master, "unshriven and unabsolved—kill not body and soul. We allow him vanquished."—"This is indeed the judgment of God," said he, looking upwards—"*Fiat voluntas tua* [62]!"

But Froissart records a most curious instance of the motives that were sometimes assigned for "a deed of arms" of this description.

Shortly after Henry IV. had ascended the throne of our feeble Richard II. Louis duke of Orleans sent him a letter of the following tenor.

"I Louis, by the grace of God, son and brother to the kings of France, duke of Orleans, write and make known to you, that with the aid of God and the blessed Trinity, in the desire which I have to gain renown, and which you in like manner should feel, considering *idleness* as the bane of lords of high birth which do not employ themselves in arms, and thinking I can no way better seek renown than by proposing to you to meet me at an appointed place, each of us accompanied with one hundred knights and esquires, of name and arms without reproach, there to combat together until one of the parties shall surrender; and he to whom God shall grant the victory, shall do with his prisoners as it may please him. We will not employ any incantations that are forbidden by the church, but make every use of the bodily strength granted us by God, having armour as may be most agreeable to every one for the security of his person, and with the usual arms; that is to say, lance, battle-axe, sword and dagger, and each to employ them as he shall think most to his advantage, without aiding himself by any bodkins, hooks, bearded darts, poisoned needles, or razors, as may be done by persons unless they be positively ordered to the contrary."

He then states, that "under the good pleasure of our Lady and my lord St. Michael" he will wait the answer of the king at Angouleme: and concludes,

"Most potent and noble prince, let me know your will in regard to this proposal, and have the goodness to send me as speedy an answer as may be; for in all affairs of arms, the shortest determination is the best, especially for the kings of France, and great lords and princes; and as many delays may arise from business of importance, which must be attended to, as well as doubts respecting the veracity of our letters, that you may know I am resolved, with God's help, on the accomplishment of this deed of arms, I have signed this letter with my own hand, and sealed it with my seal of arms. Written at my castle of Coucy, the 7th of August, 1402."

Henry replied to this curious challenge, by expressing his surprise at such an invitation from a sworn friend and ally. — "With regard to what you say, that we ought to accept your proposal to avoid idleness," he adds, "it is true we are not so much employed in arms and honourable exploits as our noble predecessors have been; but the all-powerful God may, when he pleases, make us follow their steps, and we through the indulgence of his graces have not been so idle, but that we have been able to defend our honour." He declines the meeting, at that time, principally on account of the inequality of rank between the parties, — but intimates that he shall be ready to afford all proper satisfaction to his challenger on his next visit to the continent. This affair ended in a mere war of words; but the real motive of Louis was subsequently avowed by him to be the revenging on Henry what he had "done against king Richard," the son-in-law of the king of France. "With regard to your high station," he smartly says, "I do not think the divine virtues have placed you there. God may have dissembled with you, and have set you on a throne, like many other princes, whose reign has ended in confusion; but in consideration of my own honour I do not wish to be compared with you."

An *Inquisitio post mortem*, dated in the 7th of Edward III., speaks of the tenure of the manor appertaining to the royal champion as follows: "That the manor of Scrivelsby is holden by grand sergeanty, to wit by the service of finding, on the day of coronation, an armed knight, who shall prove by his body, *if need be*, that the king is true and rightful heir to the kingdom."

It is remarkable that this important document neither prescribes the absolute appearance of the lord of the manor as knight, but only that he is bound to '*find* an armed knight' if required; nor does it describe the office as hereditary. With regard to the latter point, it would seem that possession is the entire law of the case, and we suppose the office would pass with the property by sale: with respect to the former, the honour seems to have called forth the valour of every successive lord, and princes have seldom imagined that their subjects can in such a cause overstep their duty.

Anciently, the champion rode with the royal procession from the Hall to the Abbey, and proclaimed the challenge on his way, as well as at the feast: some instances have occurred of its being repeated also in the city, as at the coronation of Henry IV. At his predecessors coronation it is remarked by Walsingham, that sir John Dimmock, being armed according to custom, came to the door of the Abbey with his attendants before the service was concluded: and that the earl marshal of the day went out to him and said, he should not have made his appearance so soon.

The fate of our recent and future champions has become of late duly regarded by law. To challenge all who should dispute the pretensions of the king is rightly enough a post of honour; to accept the challenge would always, we know, have been still more bold; but an act of parliament passed during the regency (59 Geo. III. cap. 46.) abolishes altogether the trial and actual battle; so that the champion's lands, after being held with manifest peril for centuries, have at last become a peaceable possession; and all dispute respecting the crown is of course as fully disposed of. It no longer rests on the valour of a single arm—not even on that of a Marmion, or a Dymoke.

There was another office, that of the *Lord High Steward* of England, to which in former times much authority was attached. He possessed a kind of vice-regal power on the demise of the crown and until the coronation of the rightful heir, and was a governor of the kingdom immediately under the reigning monarch, so as to be able to control or remove the judicial servants of the crown, at any time. What was once the importance of this office is still indicated by the temporary guardianship of St. Edward's crown being committed to an officer bearing this title on the day of the coronation, and his honourable place of walking immediately before the king in procession. The Earls of Leicester once enjoyed this great dignity hereditarily; through them it descended to the De Montford family, until, on the attainder of the last Earl, it was granted by Henry III. to his younger son Edmund, by whom it became transmitted to John of Gaunt, and eventually to Henry IV. while Duke of Lancaster; since which period it has been prudently suffered to merge in the crown.

The *Court of Claims* takes its origin from the ancient prerogatives of the Lord High Steward, who sat judicially in the Whitehall of the king's palace, at Westminster, to receive the applications and decide upon the claims of all those who held lands on the tenure of performing some personal service at the coronation. It is a court, in fact, exercising this part of his ancient office by commission. These services had the name of *magnum servitium*, or grand sergeanty, as being attached to the person of the king, and involve the honour of knighthood in all cases; no person under the rank of a knight, nor a minor or female tenant, being allowed to perform them.

Numerous offices occur in the list of claims, to which our limits will not allow us to pay attention. Toward him who is "every inch a king" every sort of service is supposed to confer honour; and many comparatively trivial duties have been long connected with the more substantial rights of property. The preceding offices require no recognition of the Court of Claims for their exercise; but those which follow are to be substantiated before this tribunal at each successive coronation.

The hereditary *Grand Almoner* of England is an honour attached to the barony of Bedford. Its duties are to collect and distribute certain monies at the coronation from a silver dish; which the Almoner claims for his fee, together with all the cloth on which the king walks in procession from the door of the hall at Westminster to the Abbey church.

The *Chief Butlership* is traced by authentic records into the hands of William de Albini, who came to England with William the Conqueror, and has been exercised by some of the noblest families in the country since. It is now an hereditary right of the Duke of Norfolk as Earl of Arundel, and entitles the possessor to the best gold cup and cover, with all the vessels and wine remaining under the bar, and all the pots and cups, except those of gold and silver, which shall be in the wine cellar after dinner.

In the remote periods of our history, when the assassination of princes was practised by various arts, a faithful guardian of the royal cup might well be esteemed an acquisition to the court. A "chief butler" was one of the most ancient attendants on royalty, we know from Scripture history, and, according to the same details, was instrumental in bringing about that singular revolution in the court of Egypt [63], which resulted in planting the Jews there, for the accomplishment of some of the most extraordinary purposes of God. The same kind of office seems to have been held by the Jewish chieftain Nehemiah in the court of Persia, and to have given him considerable influence in accelerating the return of his countrymen from their captivity in Babylon [64].

The *Dapifer* or *Sewer*, who, "in his surcote, with tabard, sleeves, and a hoode about his neck, and his towell above all, served the messes," or arranged the dishes on the table of the coronation feast of Elizabeth, Henry VII.'s queen, is an ancient worthy of the royal day, whose office has become extinct. If the dishes are not become more tractable, or the royal observation less nice, royal feasting has become, perhaps, less rare in modern times, and this kind of skill, therefore, more common.

The *Grand Carver* – *Grand Panniter*, or provider of bread, and the Royal *Napier*, are offices that have also become extinct, while good carving and good living have been still found at the royal table; and while the *Chief Cupbearer* has retained his office and the possession of the manor of Great Wimondley, in Hertfordshire, as his reward.

The *Chief Lardiner* is also still entitled to notice, as having the care and management of the royal larder, and being duly careful of "the remainder of beef, mutton, venison, kids, lard, and other flesh; as also the fish, salt, &c. remaining in the larder," which fall to his share of the feast. This office has been attached to the manor of Scoulton, in Norfolk, from the reign of Henry II.

Nor should we omit to notice that the Lord Mayor and Citizens of London claim a snug "seat next the cupboard, on the left side of the hall," in virtue of their right to assist the Chief Butler in his duties at the coronation feast; or that his lordship serves the king after dinner with wine in a gold cup, having the cup and its cover for a fee. It is remarkable that the city claims a right to perform the same service, and to receive a similar fee, at the coronation of our queens: but as this escaped Her Majesty's law officers in the late argument for her coronation, we will not suppose it had any connexion with the strong desire for that event at the Mansion House. The mayor, bailiffs, and commonalty of Oxford also claim to assist in the office of butlery, and receive the humbler reward of three maple cups.

With other presents—of grout or gruel, maple cups and napkins, *to* the king, gentle reader, we will suppose thou hast of late been sufficiently acquainted; but the conspicuous duty of the Barons of the Cinque Ports must not pass unnoticed.

These ports claim to furnish sixteen supporters of the royal canopy, in the following proportion, *i.e.*—Hastings, 3; Dover, 2; Hithe, 2; Rye, 2; Sandwich, 3; Rumney, 2; Winchelsea, 2. It is called in an account of the coronation of Richard I. "a silk *umbraculum*, borne on four lances:" but is now generally composed of cloth of gold, having a gilt silver bell at each of the four corners, which are supported by four staves of silver. The origin of this claim is involved in such remote antiquity, that a charter of Charles II. speaks of "the time of the contrary being never remembered to have been." We have seen that a crown, ascribed to the days of King Alfred, bore a couple of bells on its sides. These accompaniments of royal and pontifical dignity, appear to be of Eastern origin; but the modern application of them is curiously contrasted with the ancient design. At the doors of the tents or houses of grandees a bell or sonorous body was generally placed, that applicants for admission might announce *their* desires [65]: thus the Jewish High Priest wore bells round the lower border of his sacerdotal garments, "that his sound might be heard" on approaching the presence of God. It was clearly designed to indicate an application for the audience of a superior: but in the roar of cannon, the clatter of church bells, and the warm gratulations of such a people as received His Majesty on a late occasion, *what* tidings of any kind could the feeble bells of the canopy convey?

We shall notice but one other claim, that of the lord of the Isle of Man to present the king with the interesting present of two falcons on the day of his coronation. "Hawks and falcons were favourite subjects of amusement, and valuable presents in those days," says Mr. Turner [66], "when the country being much overrun with wood, all species of the feathered race must have abounded. A king of Kent begged of a friend abroad two falcons of such skill and courage as to attack cranes willingly, and seizing them to throw them on the ground. An Anglo-Saxon, by his will, gives two hawks (hafocas), and all his stag-hounds (head or hundas) to his natural lord." And similarly to this claim of the king on the lord of Man, "Ethelstan," according to this writer, "made North Wales furnish him with as many dogs as he chose, whose scent-pursuing noses might explore the haunts and coverts of the deer; he also exacted *birds* 'who knew how to hunt others along the atmosphere [67].'"

The Isle of Man was given in the reign of Henry IV. to the Northumberland family; on the forfeiture of that earldom Sir John Stanley became possessed of it, on the present tenure of presenting the kings of England with two falcons on the day of their coronation; and although the sovereignty was purchased from the Duke of Athol by the crown during the late king's reign, that nobleman still holds his manorial rights by the performance of this duty.

§ 4. Anecdotes of the Actual Ceremonies of the Coronation,

Chronologically Arranged.

Although the ceremonies of the royal investiture form a *spectacle* for the eye of the passing age, rather than a subject of historical record, presenting any thing characteristic of our monarchs, traces of the "form and body of the time" have occasionally been left by them on the page of history, which it is now our design to present to the reader.

The chief of the Anglo-Saxon kingdoms of the octarchy at the close of the eighth century was Mercia; and hither we find Pope Adrian, the friend and favourite of Charlemagne, sending two legates to enforce a new code of ecclesiastical laws, as early as A.D. 785. A synod was held in Northumbria, and another in Mercia, to receive them; but while the former kingdom first embraced Christianity [68], in the latter were first exhibited, at this time, the solemn rites of an ecclesiastical consecration in the person of Egfurth, the son of Offa, who was "hallowed to king," in the presence of his father, then reigning. This phrase of the Saxon Chronicle describes all that is now known of the mode of this early coronation; but prince Egfurth seems, in virtue of it, to have reigned conjointly with his father afterwards. It is remarkable that, although the Archbishop of Canterbury soon obtained the entire ecclesiastical precedence in the coronation of our kings [69], at this same synod of Calcuith, (Chelsey, Bucks,) it was decided that a metropolitan see should be established amongst the Mercians, taking from that of Canterbury all the territory between the Thames and the Humber; and that Adrian accordingly sent the pallium of archiepiscopal dignity to Adulph, Bishop of Lichfield. Charlemagne, who called himself in letters produced at this synod, "the most powerful of the kings of the east," gives to Offa the sounding title of "the most powerful of the kings of the west [70]." Egfurth, it would seem, was not again crowned on his accession to the entire regal authority.

There is one instance of a Northumbrian coronation, in the stormy close of that dynasty, *i.e.*, that of Eardulf, A.D. 795. This prince had a singular escape from the hands of Ethelred, his predecessor, by whom he was brought to the church door of Rippon, in Yorkshire, and as the monarch and the spectators thought, put to death. The body was carried into the choir by the monks; who, in chanting the funeral service, perceived it to breathe, dressed his wounds, and carefully preserved their future sovereign in their monastery. He was consecrated and assisted to the throne by Æanbald, Archbishop of York, and two other prelates.

A consecration of Alfred the Great, which is by many writers regarded as "regal," took place at Rome, A.D. 754, when that prince was but five years of age; and was performed by Pope Leo IV. at the request of his father. Mr. Turner supposes that Æthelwulf thus intended to designate him for his heir in preference to his elder brothers: and Mr. Lingard, that it was to secure his succession to the crown *after* his brothers, to the exclusion of their children; a conjecture that is strongly supported by the subsequent arrangements of the will of Æthelwulf, by which the minor kingdom of Kent was left to his second son, Ethelbert; and the kingdom of Wessex to Ethelbald, Ethelred, and Alfred, in order of seniority. "If there be room here for conjecture, I rather think," says Selden, "that as the unction used in the baptism of king Clovis was among the French made also by tradition to be an anointing him for king, so here the use of chrisme in confirmation (for it appears that at the same time Pope Leo confirmed king Alured,) was afterward, by mistaking, accounted for the royal unction [71]."

Malmsbury says expressly that the pope gave him "the regal unction *and* the crown;" and Robert of Gloucester

— Pope Leon hȳm blessede þe he þuder com,
And þe kȳnges crowne of þȳs lond. —

It is also to be observed that no one of his brothers, Ethelbert, Ethelbald, or Ethelred, seem to have received a regal consecration, and that we do not read of a repetition of that ceremony when Alfred himself was crowned at Winchester; — and here we leave the solution of the meaning of this ceremony to the reader.

Our next is an instance of female coronation. Æthelwulf, devotedly attached to the church, and fitted more for the cowl than the crowns she was now in the habit of bestowing, espoused, on his return from a pilgrimage to Rome, Judith, the daughter of Charles the Bold—and at the close of the marriage ceremony caused her to be crowned and anointed by the archbishop of Rheims. A regal seat was prepared for her by his side, and she received the new or disused title of Queen. This was in the year 856. To his people the marriage seems to have been as distasteful as it was in itself unnatural; the lady not having reached her 12th year, and the king being advanced in age; but the "royal makings of a queen," with which she was honoured, are said to have excited their particular displeasure. Whether this arose, as is probable, from the consecration of a female to the royal dignity being wholly unprecedented at the court of Wessex, from some apprehension on the part of his subjects that the king designed to transfer their allegiance to a female at his death, or from disgust at the recent conduct of Eadburga, who had poisoned her husband king Brichtric, must at this period be matter of pure conjecture. Clear, however, it is that some of our most respectable historians must be mistaken respecting the crime of Eadburga, causing the honour of a coronation to be "*taken from* [72]" the Saxon queens. We have no instance of a female coronation in England until so late as the year 978, in the reign of Ethelred II. [73]: that of Judith, therefore, was no revival of a discontinued custom. But a degradation of the consorts of the kings of Wessex in regard to the *title* of queen, and the right to sit in equal dignity with the king upon a throne, in consequence of the crime of Eadburga, is, perhaps, sufficiently established. Mr. Lingard, whose accuracy as an historian is entitled to the highest praise, adverts to this circumstance in the following summary of the honours of an Anglo-Saxon queen. "The consort of the cẏning was originally known by the appellation of "queen," and shared, in common with her husband, the splendour of royalty. But of this distinction she was deprived by the crime of Eadburga, the daughter of Offa, who had administered poison to her husband Brichtric, the king of Wessex. In the paroxysm of their indignation the witan punished the unoffending wives of their future monarchs by abolishing, with the title of queen, all the appendages of female royalty. Æthelwulf, in his old age, ventured to despise the prejudices of his subjects. His young consort Judith was crowned in France, and was permitted to seat herself by his side on the throne. But during several subsequent reigns no other king imitated his example: and the latest of the Anglo-Saxon queens, though they had been solemnly crowned, generally contented themselves with the modest appellation of "the lady [74].""

After king "Alfride," saith Peter Langtoft—

Kam Edward the olde,
Faire man he was and wis, stalworth and bolde.

He was distinguished for those successful inroads on the Danish possessions in Britain which resulted in the entire dominion of England being united under the sceptre of his successors.

On the same authority we learn that he "toke the croun at Saynt Poule's," London: if by this his coronation is intended, Stow and Speed contradict the poet, assigning this honour to the town of Kingston-upon-Thames. But the proclamation of the monarch in London may be the meaning of the old chronicler.

Ethelstan, the first monarch of England, was crowned at Kingston, (id est, villa regia, says an early writer), "according to the ancient laws," A.D. 924, by Athelm, archbishop of Canterbury. On this occasion, as we have before noticed, a high scaffolding was erected in the market-place of that borough, for the better exhibition of the prince and of the ceremonies to the people.

The coronations of Edmund I. and Edred, his brothers, (both of which took place at Kingston,) present nothing remarkable to our notice.

But that of Edwy, the eldest son of Edmund, was distinguished for a remarkable outrage on the person of the king. The popular account of this affair is, that the young prince had espoused a beautiful young lady of the royal blood, Elgiva, who was pronounced by the monks to be within the canonical degrees of affinity. Before his accession, therefore, she had been a source of dispute between the dignified ecclesiastics and the king. On the coronation-day he did not obtrude her claims upon the people; nor, on the contrary, would he forego his private comforts in her society. When the barons were indulging themselves in the pleasures of the feast, Edwy retired to his domestic apartments, and in the company of Elgiva and her mother, laid aside his crown and regal state. Dunstan, the aspiring abbot of Glastonbury, surmised the cause of his retreat; and taking with him his creature Odo, the nominal primate, penetrated into the interior of the palace, upbraided the prince with this untimely indulgence of his passions, and after branding his consort with the most opprobrious name of woman, brought him back with considerable personal violence into the hall [75]. Mr. Turner, our able Anglo-Saxon historian, regards the transaction as a bold attempt of Dunstan to subdue the regal power to his ambition. He represents the nobility as evincing some displeasure at the king's early departure, and the anxiety of Odo to communicate the state of their minds to Edwy. That the persons he first addressed excused themselves from undertaking this errand: and the commission devolved by a sort of general wish on Dunstan and Cynesius, a bishop, his relative. "But with the delivery of the message," he observes, "his commission must have terminated; and on the king's refusal [if he did refuse] it was his duty to have retired. As an ecclesiastic, he should not have compelled him to a scene of inebriety; as a subject, it was treasonable to offer violence to his prince [76]."

The latest, and not least able of our English historians, however, would place these events in a different light. He insists, somewhat in the spirit of the monkish writers, on this amour being highly disgraceful to the king; and while he represents it as "the scandal of the age" (whose sources, in the king's disputes with the ecclesiastics, Mr. Lingard in any other instance would have readily traced,) he states it as not altogether incredible that both Ethelgiva, the mother, and her daughter, whom he does not name, had sacrificed their honour to the equivocal ambition of *one* of them becoming queen. The nobles, he adds, accompanied their demand for the king's return with an injunction in the name of the whole assembly, for Ethelgiva to leave the court. The rest of his account does not materially differ from that of former historians. But with all the unfeigned respect for his impartiality, with which the perusal of this writer's volumes has inspired us, we cannot hold him successful in this attempt to disengage the character of Dunstan and his associates from the imputation of great indecorum.

Were the lady the king's mistress and not his wife, was a dignified ecclesiastic justified in following him into her apartments? and had the amour been ever so unbecoming, was this a species of conduct likely to detach him from it? But the story of the wife and daughter together speculating upon his affections is surely improbable in the highest degree: we know that the monkish writers, who furnish the only account we have of the transaction, would call a wife espoused in opposition to the will of the church, a mistress; and the sufferings of the young monarch from this interference with his affections, should teach us to exercise the judgment of charity on his memory.

Edgar, the successor of Edwy, surnamed "the Peaceful," his whole reign being exempt from the scourge of war, delayed his coronation for thirteen of the sixteen years to which it extended; a circumstance for which none of our historians assign a reason. The royal investiture was celebrated at last, (A.D. 973,) with great pomp at Bath, Dunstan, archbishop of Canterbury, presiding.

> "There was bliss mickle
> On that happy day
> Caused to all" —

says a poem in commemoration of the event, preserved in the Saxon Chronicle,

> "Of priests a heap,
> Of monks much crowd,
> I understand." —

The monarch, indeed, was as celebrated for his magnificence as for the talents suited to his station. From Bath he proceeded to Chester, to receive the homage of eight tributary princes, *i.e.* Kenneth, king of Scotland, Malcolm of Cumberland, M'Orric of Anglesey and the Iles, Jukil of Westmoreland, Iago of Galloway, and Howel, Dyfnwel, and Griffith, princes of Wales. A splendid procession by water introduced the ceremony. Edgar assumed his seat at the stern of the royal barge, and his tributaries taking the oars, rowed the monarch to the church of St. John; the bishops and noblemen following in their state barges, and returning the acclamations of the populace who lined the shores. The king is said to have remarked, "When my successors can command the service of the like number of princes, let them consider themselves kings [77]."

A remarkable objection was made, according to the Saxon Chronicle, to the right of Edward, the son of Edgar, to the throne, viz. that he was born before the coronation either of his father or mother [78], and the pretensions of his younger brother, Ethelred, were so successfully urged by the Queen dowager, that a convocation of the witan was held to settle the dispute [79]. Here the claim of Edward was fully admitted, and he was crowned and anointed by Dunstan, at Kingston, accordingly, in the year 975 — to be sacrificed to the ambition of his cruel stepmother, in less than four years afterwards.

Stained with the blood of its former wearer, even the ambitious prelate Dunstan "hated much to give the crown" to Ethelred II., as Robert of Gloucester informs us; he assisted, however, at his coronation, and, according to the most perfect Anglo-Saxon ritual that has come down to us, addressed some admirable counsel to the monarch on the duties of his new station. The following is a translation of the coronation oath of this period. "In the name of the Most Holy Trinity, I promise; First, that the church of God, and all Christian people, shall enjoy true peace under my government; secondly, that I will prohibit all manner of rapine and injustice to men of every condition; thirdly, that in all judgments, I will cause equity to be united with mercy, that the most clement God may, through his eternal mercy, forgive us all. Amen [80]." The ceremony was performed at Kingston, on the festival of Easter, 978.

Edmund II., surnamed Ironside, was also crowned at Kingston; he struggled nobly for seven months against the overwhelming power of the Danes, who, at the moment of his coronation, had an army of 27,000 men on board their fleet in the

Thames; and who, in the fatal field of Ashdown, extirpated almost all the old nobility of the kingdom, ere this unfortunate reign closed. This hero led them, during his short reign, into five pitched battles against the enemy.

Canute is said to have been chosen by the unanimous voice of the nation to the vacant throne; and received consecration from Levingius, archbishop of Canterbury, at London, A.D. 1016. He first surrounded the throne with regular guards, called Thing-men, for whose government he compiled a set of rules still extant. The king himself having violated one of them in a transport of passion, by slaying a private soldier, assembled the whole corps, and having referred to the law prohibiting such excesses, acknowledged his crime, descended from the throne, and demanded punishment. The Thing-men were silent, and being urged, on a promise of perfect impunity, to state their sentiments, they left the decision to the king, who adjudged himself to pay 69 talents of gold, more than nine times the ordinary pecuniary mulct in such a case.

The Scots refused homage to this prince, because he had not obtained the crown of hereditary descent; but on his assembling an army to assert his claims, they submitted: shortly after which occurred the memorable effort of his courtiers to persuade him, that the monarch of six powerful nations—England, Scotland, and Wales, Denmark, Norway, and Sweden,—could command the ocean tide to retire from his feet. Having convinced them of their folly, by making the experiment, he took the crown from his head, it is said, and placed it on the great cross in the cathedral of Winchester, refusing ever after to wear it, even on occasions of public ceremony.

At the coronation of Harold I., who in fact usurped the throne in the absence of the legitimate claimant, Hardicanute, Egilnoth, archbishop of Canterbury, refused the episcopal benediction. He placed the royal insignia on the altar, and addressing the king and his surrounding prelates, said, "There are the crown and sceptre which Canute intrusted to my charge. To you, I neither give nor refuse them, you may take them if you please; but I strictly forbid any of my brother bishops to usurp an office, which is the prerogative of my see [81]."

Edward the Confessor's name is attached to too much of the Regalia, to allow us to overlook his accession to the throne. He was crowned at Winchester, A.D. 1042, on Easter day; and being a Saxon, was hailed by the people as a native prince. The archbishop, Eadsius, read to him a long exhortation on the duties of a sovereign, and closed by reminding him of the paternal government which England enjoyed under his predecessors in the Saxon line. All our early historians dwell with great zeal on the manner in which he fulfilled these duties. He was "the good king Edward," for whose "laws" the people were always anxious, when under the subsequent despotism of the Normans, they found an opportunity of expressing their desires; and his reign, forming an interval between the Danish and Norman Conquest, was long remembered as an era of deliverance from foreign thraldom. It is principally from these feelings, that historians account for the crown itself wearing for so many ages the name of St. Edward's—St. Edward's staff, as it is called, being carried before our monarchs at their coronation, &c. The people literally applied to him that celebrated maxim of our constitution, the king can do no wrong; for, although his reign was chequered by many internal commotions, on his ministers and not on himself, was the blame uniformly cast.

This prince, however, seems to have committed a pious fraud on his good people. Being importuned by his council to marry, he espoused the daughter of the powerful Earl Godwin; to whom he privately disclosed a vow of perpetual continence under which he had bound himself: but offered to raise her to the regal seat (and she was accordingly publicly crowned as queen), on condition that he should be allowed without molestation to observe his vow. She is represented by our historians as a very learned lady.

The coronation of the unfortunate Harold II. took place on the day of the funeral of his predecessor—a striking proof of the importance attached to this ceremony at that period. But William, Duke of Normandy, having previously extorted from him an oath of fealty, protested from the first against his consecration, and in the memorable battle of Hastings caused him to pay the penalty of his life for the momentary honour.

At this point of our progress through the history of these ceremonies, it will be interesting to review briefly the political character of the Anglo-Saxon *cyning* or king. The rites in question will always derive the greatest illustration from being considered as the reflected light of ancient opinions respecting the monarchy.

The eorl and ceorl were the great distinctive appellations of noble and ignoble descent: none were or are admitted, it will be seen, to any important office in the coronation ceremonies but the former class. They were said to be "ethel-born," and every member of the royal family was an "etheling," or son of the noble, emphatically. Ere Christianity dispelled the fables of divine descent, the pedigree of the monarch was always to be traced to Woden, and after the demi-god was no longer revered, the first of earthly families and "full-born" blood was seen in him.

Yet our Anglo-Saxon ancestors unquestionably *chose* the identical member of the family whom they would acknowledge as king: the witan regularly assembled on the death of a monarch, and proceeded to the election of his successor.

"The Saxons could not comprehend," says Mr. Lingard, "how a freeman could become the dependent of another, except by his own consent: but the election rendered the cyning the lord of the principal chieftains, and through them of their respective vassals."

His revenue, derived from the fines and amercements known to the Anglo-Saxon law for crimes of every description—from territory obtained by conquest, or forfeited by treason—and from those gross bargains for obtaining the king's peace, which were only exceeded by those which purchased at this time, what was called "the peace of God," (both being an exemption for certain days, or in certain places, from the pursuit of every enemy or claimant), was far larger than that of the most powerful of the nobles who were, in fact, *his* feudal tenants, in whatever portion of lands they possessed. Thrice in the year this proud muster-roll of noble tenants was examined, *i.e.* at the festivals of Christmas,

Easter, and Whitsuntide, where they appeared before the monarch in all the pomp of state. A sort of coronation scene was at this time exhibited. The nobles renewed their homage to the monarch, who received them at once as his guests and dependents—seated on his throne, with a crown on his head, and a sceptre in each of his hands. Public officers were at this time appointed, laws, on some occasions, enacted, while for eight days it was forbidden for any man to slay, maim, or assault his enemy, or to distrain upon his debtor's lands. The return of these festivals has sometimes been mistaken by our historians for a repetition of the coronation, strictly so called [82].

The monarch exercised, as at the present time, a supreme command over the national forces. He consulted the witan, but he himself determined on, and proclaimed war or peace. He was also, as now, the supreme judge, and received appeals in person, from all the ordinary courts of judicature: the ealdormen, sheriffs, and other officers of those courts, holding their appointments at his pleasure. The intelligent reader will thus find the substantial duties of the royal office as remarkably similar at this distant period with its present functions, as the pageant of a coronation can be uniform [83].

William I. may be said to have been crowned in character as a conqueror. Christmas-day 1066, being appointed for his coronation, at Westminster, he was surrounded by his Norman barons, and a full attendance of the English nobles and prelates—when Aldred, archbishop of York, put the questions of the Recognition to his new subjects; and the bishop of Constance, who was in his train, to the Normans, The assent of both nations was given with loud acclaim. So boisterous, indeed, was their loyalty at this part of the ceremony, that the Norman soldiers of William, on the outside of the Abbey church, affected to consider the shouts as the signal of insurrection, and immediately set fire to the houses of the neighbourhood (a singular remedy for riot), and began the congenial work of plunder, to the great mortification of the king. All now became confusion in the interior of the Abbey: the Norman barons prepared for battle; the native nobles regarded themselves as victims selected for slaughter, and the king is said to have been left alone, with the ecclesiastics, to conclude the ceremony. That the shouts were but the pretext for a preconcerted attack and plunder of the people, appears but too clearly from the subsequent remonstrance of the king with the barons, whom he warned against the certain result of oppressing the English; while he strictly prohibited the soldiers from appearing at taverns, or molesting the private abodes of the citizens; and appointed a commission to enforce his regulations.

Matilda, duchess of Normandy, was not brought into England until William had fully subdued his refractory subjects—when, on Whit Sunday, 1068, she was crowned queen at Winchester, by the archbishop of York.

William Rufus, though a second son, was the Conqueror's favorite, and duly elected his successor by the prelates and barons of England. His coronation, as it was principally procured by the influence of the church, was conducted with great splendour by Lanfranc, archbishop of Canterbury, at Westminster, 20th Sept, 1087.

Of this prince the Saxon Chronicle furnishes an anecdote, of which the naval excursions of his present Majesty are calculated to remind us. While hunting in the New Forest he received intelligence of the defeat of his Norman forces by Helie de la Fleche—and would hardly suffer the messenger to conclude his tale, ere he exclaimed, "Let those that love, follow me;" and rode immediately toward the sea shore. He leaped into the first vessel that presented itself: the master remonstrating that the weather was very stormy, and the passage perilous in such a bark, "Hold thy peace," said William, "kings are never drowned [84]."

Henry I., who was near his brother at the time of his death in the New Forest, hastened to Winchester to secure the royal treasures. So precipitate was the prince on this occasion, as to neglect all care for the decent interment of William, whose body was carried in a cart to the royal city, and without any religious rites interred in the cathedral [85]. The treasurer of his predecessor seems to have been more respectful to his memory. He ventured to tell Henry that he held the money for the rightful heir, his brother Robert; and blood would have been shed but for the interference of the surrounding nobles, who overcame the scruples of the minister. Having obtained possession of the royal castle and treasures, Henry proceeded to Westminster, where on the third day after his brother's death he was crowned by the bishop of London, the see of York being vacant, and Anselm, archbishop of Canterbury, abroad.

This was the first of our monarchs who thought it needful to strengthen the attachment of his subjects to him by a formal charter; which seems in some measure to have been regarded as a condition of his election to the crown. It was, at any rate, promulgated on the day of the coronation, and is a document of no small historical importance, as professing to abolish all the grievances that had been introduced by the Norman princes, and to restore the laws of Edward the Confessor. We can only notice a few of its items. 1. The people were exempted from all taxes which they had not paid under their Saxon rulers; and the venders of base or light coin were to be punished with severity. 2. The church was reinstated in all her ancient rights, and the king engaged never to sell or farm vacant benefices, or to retain their revenues for the use of his exchequer. 3. He granted to all the barons and immediate vassals of the crown (requiring them to make the same grant to their respective tenants) the right of a free disposal of personal property: that for breaches of the peace they should not be placed as heretofore at the king's mercy, but be adjudged to pay the sums prescribed by the Saxon law; that their heirs should pay the customary reliefs for the livery of lands, and not the arbitrary compensations which had been exacted by his two predecessors; that the wardship of minors, and the custody of their lands, should be committed to their nearest relations; that neither heiresses nor widows should be compelled by the king to marry, but the daughters and female relations of noble families should be given in marriage without any impediment being offered by the crown, or any fee being required for the exercise of such liberty. He at the same time granted a very beneficial charter to the citizens of London. Two queens of this prince were successively crowned.

Stephen was the fourth monarch in succession from the Conqueror who claimed the crown without an hereditary title. Any settlement of the government was preferred by well-disposed men to the anarchy that usually succeeded the decease of a feudal sovereign: and the promptitude of this monarch, and his former popularity in the country, united with the antipathy of the people to a female reign, gave him an easy access to sovereign power. He was crowned at Winchester, by the archbishop of Canterbury, Dec, 22, 1135; stipulating in the coronation oath that he would not levy the danegelt [86] which his uncle had so frequently extorted, nor retain for his own profit the vacant benefices of the church, nor molest clerks or laymen in the possession of their woods or forests.

By a compact entered into with Stephen and the assembled barons, in the latter days of that prince, Henry II., grandson of Henry I., succeeded to the throne, and was crowned at Westminster, Dec. 19, 1154, attended by a great concourse of foreign nobility. His queen received the royal unction on Christmas-day, 1158.

During the disputes between this monarch and the celebrated Thomas à Becket, we find the king adopting a singular expedient for strengthening and perpetuating the authority of his family — the coronation of his son Henry. Historians are divided as to his design in this ceremony; but a probable opinion is suggested by Mr. Hume, that when the thunders of the Vatican were every day expected to dissolve the ties of allegiance between Henry's subjects and himself, he was anxious by the new oaths of allegiance now taken, to secure their obedience, at least, to his family in the person of his son.

But in the manner of conducting this unique coronation he added new matter to the existing strife. It had long been esteemed a right of the metropolitan to anoint and crown the kings of England; and Becket had been diligent enough to procure the pope's letters prohibitory against the interference of any other prelate with his privileges on this occasion. The coronation however proceeded; the archbishop of York feeling no scruple in supplying Becket's place: — all the royal makings of a king were bestowed on the young prince, at Westminster, June 15, 1170, and his father waited upon him during the coronation feast, at table. It being remarked to the prince how great was the honour for him to be thus attended, he is said to have replied haughtily, "That he thought it no such great condescension for the son of an earl to wait on the son of a king."

This coronation also involved the father in a rupture with the court of France. Prince Henry had married a daughter of that crown, to which the omission of her coronation with her husband was in the highest degree offensive: the king of France entered the Norman territories of Henry in consequence, and it was not until that monarch had promised to supply the omission, and that the prince and princess should be together crowned by Becket, that either the French king or the primate were appeased. The ultimate issue of this circumstance, in the assassination of Becket, we have noticed in another part of this work. Hume remarks on the whole affair—"There prevailed in that age an opinion which was akin to its other superstitions, that the royal unction was essential to the exercise of royal power. It was therefore natural both for the king of France, careful of his daughter's establishment, and for Becket, jealous of his own dignity, to demand in the treaty with Henry some satisfaction on this essential point [87]." The second coronation of the prince (in which his consort was duly associated) took place Aug. 27th, 1172.

Nor did the calamitous consequences of this event thus terminate. It seems to have sown deeply the seeds of ambitious discord in the family of Henry. The young prince, after a visit to France with his consort, formally demanded of his father some substantial share of the royal power with whose insignia he had been invested. The intrigues and civil commotions that followed, it is not within our plan to detail; but the conduct of his different children, instigated by the example of this unworthy first-born, eventually brought the parent to his grave.

The coronation of Richard I., is the earliest upon which our historians dilate. It took place September 3, 1189, at Westminster; differing in no material point from the modern ceremony. The archbishop is said to have solemnly adjured the king at the altar, "not to assume the royal dignity unless he were resolved to keep the regal oath." An infamous outrage on the unoffending and oppressed race of the Jews closed the coronation day in London, and was followed by equally cruel treatment of them in several large towns. They seem on this occasion to have tempted the cupidity, by appealing to the generosity and humanity of the court. Numbers of them came to the metropolis with presents for the young king, who forbade them, however, to appear at his coronation. In the evening a few of the richer Israelites endeavoured to pass into the hall of the palace; when they were repulsed, insulted, and pursued into the city. A report now spread that the king, regretting the unhallowed forbearance of his father toward this apostate race, had given orders for a general attack upon them. The populace quickly murdered the first that had appeared; they then attacked the houses of all the richer Jews, and after stripping them of every thing valuable, left them in flames. At York, five hundred of this hapless nation who had retired into the castle for protection, and eventually seized it from the governor, murdered their own wives and children, to prevent their falling into the hands of their enemies, and then despatched each other nearly to a man.

On the return of Richard from his romantic expedition to Jerusalem, in 1194, he is said to have been crowned a second time; "to put awaie, as it were, the reproofe of his captivitie [88]." A solemn council was held at Nottingham, to review the affairs of the kingdom, and the conduct of his brother John during the king's absence; the last or third day being occupied in discussing the question, whether it were necessary that the king should be crowned a second time; the king voted in the negative, but his peers and prelates were of the contrary opinion, and the ceremony was accordingly performed at Winchester, by Hubert, archbishop of Canterbury [89].

John was declared by Richard, on his death-bed, to be his legitimate successor: but the people being divided between his claims and those of Arthur, his nephew, a great council was held at Northampton, in which the nobles resolved unanimously on swearing fealty to him; and the coronation was ordered to take place at Westminster, 27th of May, 1199. The primate introduced the ceremony by a speech intended to maintain the claim of John. He observed, that all his auditors well knew the crown to be elective, and could only be held by the unanimous agreement of the nation with regard to the personal merits of the wearer: that it was the gift of the people, who chose generally from the members of the reigning family the prince who appeared most deserving of that honour. Such was the selection in the scriptural case of David, and others: and that having that day met to perform this important duty, they, on these principles, brought forward their future sovereign, John, earl of Montaigné, brother to the deceased king [90]. John, who was present, signified his concurrence with these sentiments; and a few days afterwards, (June 7) we find a law published from Northampton in which he asserts, that 'God had given him the throne by hereditary right, through the unanimous consent and favour of the clergy and people [91].' The friends of Arthur made a faint resistance to the claims of John, as duke of Normandy, but that unhappy prince, we know, soon met an untimely death, by the means, if not by the dagger of his uncle.

This prince, having procured a divorce, on the pretext of consanguinity, from a wife to whom he had been married twelve years, negociated a new marriage in 1200 with the princess of Portugal. Ere his overtures, however, could be answered, he was by accident diverted to another choice. Isabella, daughter of the count of Angouleme, was a celebrated beauty of the day, who had been publicly promised and privately espoused to Hugh, count of La Marche. But John, in one of his visits to Normandy, became enamoured of her: and the lady found the crown of her new lover an irresistible recommendation. The princess of Portugal was disappointed, the count de La Marche enraged, and all Europe surprised at the event, when the monarch conducted his bride in triumph to Westminster early in the month of October, and assembled his peers for her coronation, on the 8th of that month. Hoveden represents king John himself to have partaken of the benediction on the occasion: some writers state, that he was a second time crowned.

Soon after this event, we have a formal demand of feudal

homage made by John on William king of Scotland, with which the latter promised promptly to comply. The two monarchs met at Lincoln, and, on an eminence near that city, in the presence of the assembled nobles of both kingdoms, the king of Scotland swore fealty of life and limb to John—against all men, saving his own right. He, at the same time, is said to have acknowledged by a written document the feudal superiority of the English crown, to have engaged to keep the peace with its king and kingdom, and to have bound himself not to marry his son without the permission of John, as his liege lord [92]. But this is a little inconsistent with another recorded fact—rising from his knees, he explicitly demanded of John the restoration of the three counties of Northumberland, Cumberland and Westmoreland, as the heir of his grandfather David, from whom he alleged them to have been unjustly wrested in the wars of Matilda and Stephen. The kind of homage rendered by the Scottish princes to the English crown, in this and succeeding ages, was always proportioned to the strength or weakness of the respective governments, and was hardly construed to mean the same thing during two successive reigns. On the whole, this singular interview seems to have been consented to on the part of the wily Scot, principally with a view to sound the dispositions of the new sovereign.

The profligate and pusillanimous John is well known to have exposed his own rights, and the liberties of his people, to all the evils of protracted civil wars, and foreign invasion. At the period of his decease, the capital and the southern counties were in the hands of Louis, king of France.

Henry III., his son, had but just completed his tenth year when the title of a king descended to him. But his youth and innocence conciliated that regard to his person, which the conduct of John had long estranged from himself; the claims of Louis were disowned by the holy see; and the more powerful of the barons saw an object worth contending for in the direction of the young king's affairs. Ten days after the death of his father, (October 28, 1218), he was brought in procession to the cathedral of Gloucester, and crowned by the papal legate Gualo, assisted by the bishops of Winchester, Exeter, and Bath. It is remarked by the contemporary historians [93], that a plain circle of gold was used on this occasion in lieu of the crown, which had been lost with the other jewels and baggage of John in his passage across the wash near Wisbech. A proclamation was next day issued, lamenting the dissensions that had existed between the king's father and his barons, and promising, on the part of Henry, to bury them in oblivion. By the same instrument he commanded the tenants of the crown forthwith to appear, and do him homage; and enjoined upon all persons appearing in public, to wear a white fillet round their heads during the ensuing month, in honour of his coronation.

Henry was crowned a second time, on the final deliverance of his kingdom from the French invaders, *i.e.* in May 1220; by Langton, archbishop of Canterbury: — "all the estates and subjects of his realme," meeting him at Westminster — "to the end; it might be said, that now after the extinguishment of all seditious factions, he was crowned by the general consent [94]."

At the late age of twenty-nine, a bride was provided for the young monarch: her father, who accompanied her to England, was only bishop elect of Valence; but the beauty of the queen seems in this case to have been the sovereign recommendation; and all the eloquence of the historian is exerted by Matthew Paris, in describing the ceremonies of her marriage and coronation. The nobility of both sexes, the clergy in their various orders, all the vassals of the crown and the citizens are assigned their several places and offices, with an amusing precision; nor does he forget the trumpet's clang, or the minstrel's pipe: the various banners that streamed in the procession; or the viands and wines of the banquet. Eleanor, the pride of the day, was a queen amongst beauties — the whole world, he says in conclusion, might be challenged to produce a spectacle equally glorious and enchanting.

This monarch rebuilt the whole of the abbey church at Westminster from its foundations; and was interred in the tomb out of which he had removed the bones of Edward the Confessor. At his funeral his successor was proclaimed by the earl of Gloucester; who, before the deceased king's body was covered, stept forward, and putting his hand upon it, swore fealty to the then absent prince.

Edward I., at this period returning to Europe from the Holy Land. He is said to have received the news of his father's death with those tears of sincere grief, which surprised some of his princely companions; and did not much appear to quicken his progress toward England. Being challenged to a tournament, by the count of Chalons, the exhortations of the reigning Pontiff could not induce him to forego the combat; he felt his honour, as the champion of the cross, at stake; and appeared in the lists at the appointed day, attended by a thousand knights. The trial of skill was converted into a deadly battle, in which the count seriously attempted the king's life; and out of which, the English only came victorious after a sanguinary conflict. Edward succeeded to the throne in November 1272; but did not arrive in England, until August 1274, when his first object was to receive, with his consort, Eleanor of Castile, the regal unction. He was crowned with this affectionate [95] companion of his crusade, at Westminster, on the 19th; Alexander, king of Scotland, being present, and doing homage as a vassal of the English crown. Several of the orders for provisions required for the coronation feast, are preserved in Rymer, among which are, 380 head of cattle; 430 sheep, 450 pigs, 18 wild boars, 278 flitches of bacon; and 19,660 capons and fowls. Holinshed informs us, that there were five hundred horses "let go at libertie" on this occasion, "catch them that catch might." In Rymer we also read of a singular stipulation originally made by Richard I., that, whenever a king of Scotland should attend at the summons of the English king, to do homage, or service at his court, he should be attended, and provided for, by the bishop, sheriffs, and barons of each county, through which he came; 5*l.* per day being allowed for his expenses on the road, and 30*s.* per day so long as he remained at the English court, together with twenty-four loaves, four sexterces of the best, and eight of inferior, wine, four wax tapers, forty better, and eighty inferior, candles, two pounds of pepper, and four pounds of cinnamon. At this time, it appears, the Scottish party received regularly the 5*l.* a day, and purchased their own provision: Alexander's whole disbursement was 175*l.*

Edward, in the first year after his coronation, forbade the Jews to erect, or hold any synagogues in his dominions; to hold fiefs, or any free tenement; or to demand interest for the loan of money: at seven years of age they were to wear two pieces of woollen cloth, sown into their outward garment, and at twelve to be subject to a capitation tax of three pence, to be paid annually at Easter. Thus cut off from their ordinary modes of living, they had recourse to the clipping of money and other illegal modes of debasing the coin; and after trials, fines, and executions of the most oppressive and unjustifiable description, were finally banished the realm, A.D. 1290.

Edward II. ascended a throne that, by the energies of his father, had extended its sway over almost the whole island of Great Britain. At the period of his decease, Edward I. was prosecuting the conquest of Scotland, and left, according to Froissart, a solemn charge to his successor, "to have his body boiled in a large cauldron, until the flesh should be separated from the bones; that he would have the flesh buried and the bones preserved; and that every time the Scots should rebel against him, he would summon his people, and carry against them the bones of his father: for he believed most firmly, that as long as his bones should be carried against the Scots, those Scots should never be victorious [96]." The young prince first visited the court of France, and married Isabella, the French king's daughter; whom he brought to England with her two uncles, and a magnificent train of foreign nobility, to participate in the splendors of their joint coronation, which was celebrated at Westminster, February 25, 1308. It was well attended also by the English nobility; but the king's marked preference for a personal favourite, (Piers Gaveston) was resented as a general insult. He appeared the sole dispenser of all the honours and favours of the day; for the promotion of his friends and dependents, the claims of inheritance and the precedents of former reigns were alike disregarded. Three days afterwards, the barons met in the refectory of the monks, at Westminster, to petition for the banishment of Gaveston, and thus began the unhappy differences between this monarch and his nobles, which resulted in his final deposition.

This involved the singular circumstance of the barons formally withdrawing their homage. The favourites of the king, against whom they had armed, being slain,—a parliament was called by the queen Isabella, and *her* paramour; which was opened by a long speech from the bishop of Hereford. He painted in strong terms the incapacity, and what he called the vindictive and treacherous disposition, of the king; and declared, that to liberate him from the confinement under which he was now placed, would be to expose to certain death, a princess, who, by her wisdom and courage, had been the salvation of the state. He, therefore, desired them to retire, and to consider, by the next morning, whether it were not better to deprive the father of the crown, and elect, forthwith, his son. On the following day this motion was carried by acclamation; the temporal peers, and many of the prelates, swore fealty at once to the young Edward: a bill of impeachment, containing six articles, was drawn up against the old king; and the reign of Edward of Carnarvon was declared to have terminated, and that of Edward of Windsor to have begun.

But the queen now affected great scruples and grief at these proceedings; declared her fears, that the parliament had exceeded its powers, and exhorted her son, it is said, to refuse the crown. On the ground of this delicacy of feeling, a deputation of both lords and commons was appointed to wait on the deposed monarch,—to give him notice of the election of his son; tender him back their homage, and "act as circumstances might suggest." Their measures are variously related by the partisans of the new and old king. They flattered and they threatened him; they exhorted him to show that greatness of mind, which could sacrifice a throne to the good of his people, and promised him an ample revenue and the indulgence of all his personal wishes, if he should freely resign the crown. At last he was brought, dressed in a plain black gown, into a room where the deputation had been arranged to receive him; and sir William Trussel, a judge, addressed him in these words: "I, William Trussel, procurator of the earls, barons, and others, having for this full and sufficient power, do render and give back to you Edward, once king of England, the homage and fealty of the persons named in my procuracy:

and acquit and discharge them thereof, in the best manner that law and custom will give. And I now make protestation, in their name, that they will no longer be in your fealty, or allegiance, nor claim to hold any thing of you as king, but will account you, hereafter, as a private person, without any manner of royal dignity." Then sir Thomas Blount, the steward of the king's household, broke his staff of office, as is usual on the death of a king, and declared all persons once in his Majesty's service, to be discharged from their former duty.

On the return of the deputation, the new king was proclaimed in the metropolis by the heralds, in the following unprecedented form. "Whereas, sir Edward, late king of England, of his own good will, and with the common advice and assent of the prelates, earls, barons, and other nobles, and all the commonalty of the realm, hath put himself out of the government of the realm, and has granted and willed that the government of the said realm should come to sir Edward, his eldest son and heir, and that *he* should govern the kingdom, and be crowned king, on which account all the lords have done him homage; we cry and publish the peace of our said lord, sir Edward, the son, and on his part strictly command and enjoin under pain and peril of disherison and loss of life and member, that no one break the peace of our said lord the king. For he is, and will be ready to do justice to all and each of the said kingdom, both to the little and the great, in all things and against all men. And if any one have a claim against another, let him proceed by way of action, and not by violence or force."

At the coronation, February 1st, 1327, a similar assertion of the late king having resigned by his free-will, and with the consent of parliament, was made. The medal distributed during the ceremony, represented the son resting his sceptre on the heart of his people, within the motto, "Populo dat jura volenti;" having on the reverse a hand receiving a fallen crown, with the inscription, "Non rapit, sed recipit." The best comment on the "free-will" of the deposed monarch, appeared in his being murdered by the queen's party, in the course of the year following.

Edward III. married Philippa of Hainault, in 1327, on which

occasion she was crowned at Westminster. She bore the king a son, the celebrated Edward the Black Prince, before he had reached his 19th year.

Richard II. succeeded his grandfather in 1377, being then in his eleventh year; and no coronation in our annals was more magnificent. The Liber Regalis, still preserved at Westminster, contains the ritual used on this occasion, and a record of the proceedings of the Court of Claims is also extant [97].

On the day after the death of Edward, this prince entered London in great state: triumphal arches were erected, conduits ran with wine, and the usual pageants of the coronation procession were displayed in the streets. Walsingham mentions in particular a turreted building, erected in the market of Cheap, out of which ran streams of wine, and at the angles of which, on the top, four young maidens of the age of the king were placed, dressed in white. On the approach of the sovereign, shreds of gold leaf were blown to him, and florins *of paper* were showered on his head! — such was what at this time was regarded as the "superior ingenuity of the merchants of Cheapside."

The progress through the city on the day preceding the coronation, (15th of July, 1377) was similarly distinguished. The king dined at the Tower, from which he came forth dressed in white garments, and placed himself under the escort of the mayor and citizens, who conducted him to his palace at Westminster. On the following morning he rose early, and, having received mass in his private chapel, came down into the great hall "arraid in the fairest vestments, and with buskins only upon his feet." The procession from Westminster Hall to the Abbey, was now marshalled in the usual order. While the litany was chanted the young prince lay prostrate before the altar, whence he was conducted to his throne on a platform in the centre of the nave. The entire ceremony of the coronation so much exhausted him, that he was borne back to the palace in a litter carried by knights. He soon, however, appeared at the banquet, where he created four earls and nine knights, and partook of a splendid though turbulent repast. The next morning a council of regency was formed, to exercise the royal authority, during the minority of the king. It is remarkable, that in the first parliament of this monarch's reign, we find the archbishop of Canterbury recommending the young king to the affection of his subjects, because he was not an elected sovereign, but the true heir and representative of their former kings [98].

On the 22d of January, 1382, this monarch espoused Anne of Bohemia, daughter of the late emperor Charles IV., and sister of Winceslaus, king of the Romans. As usual, she was crowned at the same period; and is said so entirely to have possessed, during the twelve years of her union with him, the affections of her husband and his people, as to be long remembered among the latter by the title of the good Queen Anne.

The tragic close of this prince's reign will never be forgotten while

– – – – "The hallowed crown
Shall round the mortal temples of a king,"

or Shakspeare's celebrated "Richard II." be extant. The march of his successor, Bolingbroke, from Ravenspur to London, and the rapid increase of his followers from twenty men to sixty thousand, his peaceful entry into the metropolis, and ultimate possession of the kingdom, without striking a blow, have only been exceeded, in modern times, by the celebrated march of Napoleon from Cannes to Paris.

Henry IV. challenged the crown partly by right of conquest [99]. In his coronation, which took place on the 13th of Oct. 1399, he caused the sword which he wore when he landed at Ravenspur to be carried naked, on his left hand, by the earl of Northumberland. Froissart's description of "the progress" of this monarch we have before noticed.

Of Henry V., Holinshed says, "This kyng, this man, was he whiche, (accordyng to the old proverbe) declared and shewed that honour ought to change maners: for incontinent after that he was stalled in the siege royall, and had received the crowne and sceptre of this famous and fortunate region, [he] determined with hymself to put on the shape of a new man, and to use another sorte of livyng, turning insolence and wildnesse into gravitie and sobernes, and wavering vice into constant virtue." It was this prince, our readers will recollect, who, while "the immediate heir of England," was committed into custody by the Lord Chief Justice, for disturbing the court in which he sat as judge, and who afterwards, when king, so nobly commended that officer's conduct. Shakspeare has a similar train of thought with the old chronicler.

> — —"Princes all, believe me, I beseech you,
> My father is gone wild into his grave;
> For in his tomb lie my affections;
> And with his spirit sadly I survive,
> To mock the expectations of the world,
> To frustrate prophecies, and to raze out
> Rotten opinion, which hath writ me down
> After my seeming. Though my tide of blood
> Hath proudly flowed in vanity till now;
> Now doth it turn and ebb unto the sea,
> Where it shall mingle with the state of flood,
> And flow henceforth in formal majesty [100]."

Fabian gives a splendid account of the coronation of Katherine, the queen of Henry V. "upon whose ryght hande satte at the ende of the same table the archebyshop of Cauntorbury, and Henrye, surnamed the ryche cardynall of Wynchester. And vppon the lefte hande of the quene satte the Kynge of Scottes in hys estate, the wyche was served wythe covered messe, like vnto the forenamed byshoppes, but after them." "And ye shall vnderstande, that this feaste was al of *fyshe*." Each course had its "sotyltye," however, embodying the wit of other parts of the creation; as "a pellycane syttyng on his nest with her byrdes, and an ymage of saynte Katheryne holdyng a boke and disputyng with the doctoures, holdyng a reason in her ryghte hande, saiynge: 'Madame le roigne' and the pellycan as an answere, 'Ce est la signe et du roy, partenir joy, et a tout sa gent, elle mete sa entent,'—a sotyltye named a panter with an ymage of saynte Katheryne with a whele in her hande, and a rolle wyth a reason in that other hande, sayeng: 'La royne ma file, in ceste ile, per bon reson, aves renoun.'" &c.

Henry VI. had the high honour of being solemnly crowned as king, both at London and in Paris—"in infant bands." In the ninth year of his age "he was leyde upon the high scaffold" in Westminster Abbey, "and that was covered all with red soy between the high autere and the quere. And he was set in his astate in the middes of the scaffold there, beholdynge the people all abowte sadly and wisely." The archbishop "made a proclamacion on the iiij quarters of the scaffolde, seyend in this wyse: Sirs, heere comyth Henry, kyng Henryes sone the Vth, on whos sowle God have mercy, amen. He homblyth hym to God and to holy cherche, askynge the crowne of this reame by right and defence of herytage; if ye hold ye pays with hym, say ya, and hold up handes. And than all the people cryed with oon voyce, Ye, ye. Having been crowned, he rose vp ayen and wente to the shryne; and there was he dyspoyled of all his bysshopp's gere, and arayd as a kynge in rich cloth of gold, with a crowne on his hede; which crown the kyng dyd doo make for hymself [101]." The following account of the appearance of the champion at the coronation feast, will show the antiquity of the present observances. "Settynge at the mete the kyng kept his astate; and on the right hand sat the cardynall with a lower astate, and on the left hande satt the chaunceler and a bysshop of Fraunce, and no mob at that table. And on the righth hand of the table at that boord sat the barons of the V. portes. And so forth the clerkes of the same chauncery. And on the lefte hande of the hall sat the mayre of London with the aldyrmen. And so forth worthy cominers: and in the myddes of the hall sat the bisshoppes, justices, and worthy knyghts and equyers. And so they filled bothe the midde boordes of the hall. And upon a scaffold stoode the kynges herawdes of armes all the tyme with crownes on thyr hedes; and at the fyrst cours they came down from her scaffold, and they wente before the kynges champyon Sir Phelip Dymok that rode in the hall bright as saynte George! And he proclaimed in the iiij quarters of the hall that the kyng was a rightfull kyng and heyre to the crowne of Engelond: and what maner man that wyll say the contrary he was redy to defende it as hys knyght and hys chaumpion, for by that offyce he holdith his lande [102]."

At Paris, in his eleventh year, this prince was "honourably accompanied to the church of our Lady, where he was anointed and crowned by the cardinal bishop of Winchester, after which he departed to the palace, having one crown on his head, and another borne before him." "But what should I speake," continues Grafton, "of the honorable service, the dayntie dishes, the pleasant conceytes, the costly wynes, the sweet armony, the musicall instruments which were seene and shewed at that feast, sithe all men may conjecture, that nothing was omitted that might be bought for golde, nor nothing was forgotten, that by man's wyt could be invented [103]."

Our fourth Edward, like John, affected an elective right to the crown. What is now called the Recognition, being at this period what Burnet terms, "a rite of an election, rather than a ceremony of investing one, who was already king." "A question was asked of the people then present," says Fabian, "if they would admitte hym for their kyng and soveraigne lorde, the which with one voice cried Yea, yea."

Richard III. and his consort Anne, were crowned with great state at Westminster, 6th of July, 1483; there being an unusual concourse of nobility at this festival, according to Walpole, including three duchesses of Norfolk. Some preparations seem also to have been made for the appearance of his deposed nephew, Edward V., in the procession, but whether he in reality wore his "apparel and array" there, will ever remain, among "Historic Doubts." The circumstance of such an arrangement being publicly made, however, demonstrates the confidence of Richard in his own title. Lord Orford, who first brought forward the evidence of this singular arrangement, says, "Though Richard's son did not walk at his father's coronation, Edward V. probably did. I conceive all the astonishment of my readers at this assertion, and yet it is founded on strongly presumptive evidence. In the coronation roll itself, is this amazing entry: 'To lord Edward, son of late king Edward IV., for his apparel and array, that is to say, a short gowne made of two yards and three quarters of crymsyn clothe of gold, lined with two yards and three quarters of blac velvet, a long gowne made of six yards of crymsyn cloth of gold, lynned with six yards of green damask, a shorte gowne made of two yards and three quarters of purpell velvet, &c.' Let nobody tell me that these robes, this magnificence, these trappings for a cavalcade, were for the use of a prisoner. Marvellous as the fact is, there can be no doubt but the deposed young king walked, or it was intended should walk, at his uncle's coronation [104]."

Henry VII. was crowned "both in form and substance" on Bosworth Field. Grafton's remark is, "Lord Stanley took the crown of king Richard, which was found amongst the spoyle in the field, and set it on the erle's head — as though he had been *elected* king by the voyce of the people, as in auncient tymes past in divers realmes it hath been accustomed [105]." This monarch, it is well known, endeavoured to strengthen the substantial claims of conquest by those of marriage with the daughter of Edward IV., and his own hereditary rights. To the people, he seems to have promised a joint coronation with "dame Elizabeth his wief," according to a "Little Devise" of his coronation at Westminster, which has reached the present times. But in point of fact, she did not appear there. Unwilling to lose the influence, Henry was still more determined not to appear to rely on the importance, of his matrimonial title: he did not, therefore, marry the heiress of the house of York, until after his coronation, and delayed to invest her with the diadem, until the 3d year of his reign. We have a fine description of her coronation in Mr. Ives' Select Papers relating to English Antiquities, to which we have already adverted.

No English monarch ascended the throne under happier auspices, or with more splendour, than Henry VIII. "The ordre of the services" of this "high and honourable coronation" is given at great length by Hall: in which the disused custom of a progress through the metropolis constitutes no small part of the pageantry.

Katherine of Arragon appeared on this occasion, borne on a litter by two white palfreys, "apparelled in white satyn embroudered, her heeire hanging doune to her back of a very great length, bewtefull and goodly to behold, and on her head a coronate set with many rich orient stones." The entrance of the champion, and his challenge, are in the highest style of feudal pomp, and in strict accordance with the old mode of trial by combat. "The seconde course beyng served, in at the haule doore entered a knight, armed at al poyntes, his bases rich tissue embroudered, a great plume and a sumpteous of ostriche fethers on his helmet, sittyng on a great courser trapped in tissue, and embroudered with tharmes of England, and of Fraunce, and an herauld of armes before him. And passyng through the halle, presented hymself with humble reverence before the kynges majestie, to whom garter kyng of herauldes cried and said, with a loude voyce, Sir knight, from whence come you, and what is your pretence? This knight's name was Sir Robert Dimmocke, champion to the kyng by tenure of his enheritaunce, who answered the saied kyng of armes in effecte after this manner:—Sir, the place that I come from is not materiall, nor the cause of my repaire hether is not concernyng any matter of any place or countrey, but only this; and therewithall commanded his heraulde to make an O yes: then saied the knyght to the kyng of armes, Now shal ye here the cause of my commyng and pretence. Then he commaunded his owne herauld by proclamacion to saye: If there be any persone, of what estate or degree soever he be, that wil saie or prove that King Henry the Eight is not the rightfull enheritor and kyng of this realme, I, Sir Robert Dimmocke, here his champion, offre my glove, to fight in his querrell with any persone to the utteraunce."

The coronation of Anne Boleyn was distinguished by the appearance of "marvailous connyng pageauntes" in the city: all the Graces were seen on Cornhill; the Muses hailed her approach "in Cheap;" and the Cardinal Virtues (how are times changed!) paraded Fleet Street. At the banquet the king took his station, incog. in a little closet made out of the cloyster of St. Stephen's, on the right side of the hall.

We are informed by Burnet, that at the coronation of Edward VI. the office for that ceremony was revised and much shortened; there being "some things that did not agree with" the existing "laws of the land, as the promise made to the abbotts for maintaining their lands and dignities;" and "for the tedious length of the same, which should weary and be hurtsome, peradventure, to the king's majesty, being yet of tender age, fully to endure and bide out [106]."—"The most material thing in it," he adds, "is the first ceremony, whereby the king being shewed to the people at the four corners of the stage, the archbishop was to demand their consent to it; and yet in such terms as to demonstrate he was no elective prince, for he being declared the rightful and undoubted heir, both by the laws of God and man, they were desired to give their good wills and assent to the same, as by their duty and allegiance they were bound to do." Yet 'King Edward's Journal,' preserved in the Appendix of this writer, says, "and it was asked of the people whether they would have him *to be the king*? Who answered, yea, yea." The young monarch did not, of course, understand the doctrine of his own "legitimacy" so well as his loyal courtiers.

Mary, our first queen regnant, was crowned at Westminster, Oct. 1, 1553, by Gardiner, bishop of Winchester; the archbishops of Canterbury and York being both involved in the rigorous persecution of the Protestants which had now begun. In Cheapside the chamberlain of the city presented her majesty with a purse containing a thousand marks of gold. It is somewhat remarkable, that with all the personal fondness of Mary for her husband, Philip of Spain, she should never have proposed his coronation, in any form: it would have been quite as regular and constitutional, we imagine, as that of a queen consort, and much more so than many of her fruitless efforts to promote his influence and authority over her subjects.

Queen Elizabeth, according to the usual custom, resorted to the Tower at the death of her sister. Every part of her conduct, until finally established in the most unbounded sway over the hearts of her people, is from this moment interesting. On entering the Tower she is said to have been immediately impressed with the important change that had taken place in her condition since she was imprisoned in that fortress, and in constant danger of her life. She went on her knees in gratitude to Heaven, and spoke of her deliverance being as great as that of Daniel from the lions' den: an "act of pious gratitude," says Hume, "which seems to have been the last circumstance in which she remembered any past hardships or injuries." Cautious and temperate as she was in the restoration of Protestantism, the prelates almost entirely refused to grant her episcopal consecration. At length, Oglethorpe, bishop of Carlisle, was prevailed upon to officiate—but he was the only bishop present.

Whether the solemn presentation of the Bible to the sovereign, at his coronation, was an improvement upon the pageant in which an English Bible was presented to this princess during her progress through the city (see p. 60), or at which of our Protestant coronations it was introduced, we know not. It clearly is a Protestant and most appropriate symbol of the royal duty, and of the best means of performing it.

In her first communication with her parliament, there is an allusion of this princess to one part of the coronation ceremony, which we must not omit to notice. The Commons, after granting a liberal subsidy, ventured to recommend the queen to marry. In reply she told them, that as the application was general, without presuming to direct her choice as to a husband, she could not take offence at it; but that any further interposition on their parts would have ill become them to make, or her to bear: that even while she was a private person, and exposed to much danger from the malice of her enemies, she had always declined that engagement, as an encumbrance; much more at present must she persevere in that sentiment, when the charge of a great kingdom was committed to her, and her life ought to be devoted to its interests: that as *England* was her husband, wedded to her by this pledge (and here she exhibited her finger with the coronation ring upon it), Englishmen were her children; and while she was employed in rearing or governing such a family, she could not deem herself barren, or her life useless and unprofitable: that if she ever entertained thoughts of changing her condition, the care of her subjects' welfare would be uppermost in her thoughts; but should she live and die a virgin, she doubted not but divine Providence, seconding their counsels and her own measures, would be able to prevent all dispute with regard to the succession;—and that, for her part, she desired no higher character or fairer remembrance of her should be transmitted to posterity, than to have this inscription engraved on her tombstone, "Here lies Elizabeth, who lived and died a maiden queen!"

The accession of James I. to the throne was distinguished by nothing remarkable connected with our subject, except the numerous creations of peers and other titles. He is said, during the first six weeks after his entrance into the kingdom, to have bestowed knighthood on 237 persons. It was at this period that an advertisement was affixed to the door of St. Paul's cathedral, offering to teach a new art of memory, to enable the people to recollect the names of the additions to the nobility.

There has been a recent publication of Sir Edward Walker's "Account of the Preparations for the Coronation of King Charles II.;" but his "minute detail" adds nothing important to the history of that splendid ceremony, unless we so account the "double felicitie" of the prince and people, "that as hee was the object of innumerable multitudes of his subjects, so by no accident from Towre-Hill to his own palace, no one suffered the least prejudice; and that the sunne shined gloriously all that day and the next until after his coronation, not one drop of raine falling in all that time, as very much had done at least ten dayes before, and as many after those two great solemnityes [107]."

Sandford, the "most dutiful author and collector" of the details of James II.'s coronation, has furnished the only complete text-book of our subject. Mr. Taylor, and all subsequent writers, follow him throughout the entire ritual of the church service, and in "every thing relating to practice [108]." In an address to "the King," he speaks of "the pomp, the dignity, and the many glorious circumstances which accompany this matter and occasion," "being such as would *endanger the tempting* of another man to swell a dedication to the bulk of a History;" and dilates upon "the boundless antiquity of the imperial descent," with the splendour, "both in war and peace," of the kingly progenitors of His Majesty—not forgetting the "*series of miracles*," which he asserts to have been still following in that descent, and to have been specially "wrought in favour of His Majesty's life and government." "If I should presume to follow the impulse of my zeal," he adds, "I should *enlarge* myself upon this theme; but being conscious, that it is as little my faculty as it is my province, and that long importunities from a subject to his sovereign are neither good discretion nor good manners; I will take care not to be needlessly troublesome, by being over officiously thankful," &c. This is modest enough for the introduction of a folio on the royal occupations of one day.

The book describes the preparations for the coronation, the performances, and the subsequent claims arising out of the performances of the day: but it is as stiff and stately throughout as in the dedication. Omitting no one Christian name of a dowager peeress, nor of any "individual person who went in the grand proceeding," nor even of "such who *ought* to have gone," it furnishes not a single personal anecdote of the day, nothing that stirs our sympathies: the king is a sort of demi-god, "most high, most mighty, and most excellent," and his nobles a number of well ordered automata moving round him. They speak all the day "out of a book held before" them. Nothing is heard, even at dinner, but grace and defiance from the bishop and champion.

Something human, however, appears in their appetites. In the Journal of Preparations, we find His Majesty's pleasure declared in council, that "a particular account" should be obtained "of the dinner kept in Westminster Hall, at the coronation of His Majesty King Charles II., as also that provided at the coronation of his royal father; together," gentle reader, "with the whole *expense* and charge of the said dinners." And we accordingly find the feet and inches of the royal table of Charles II. duly given; the courses of meat, hot and cold, and the dishes in each course; as likewise the orders of the "*banquet*," served in plate, on each of the tables of the Hall: that term (our future commentators on Shakspeare must observe) being confined to the "confections dried and wet, with fruit of the season." In another minute of council is a recommendation that there "be provided a magnificent table for their Majesties in the nature of an ambigue; but with two courses, in regard to the ceremonies that are to be performed at the second course." On turning to our books to understand *this* method of good living, we were somewhat startled to find the following contradictory recommendation, quoted by Johnson, from an old Art of Cookery:—

> When *straitened* in your time, and servants *few*,
> You'd richly then compose an ambigue,
> Where first and second course, and your desert,
> All in *one single* table have their part.

St. George's day, in 1684-5, was happily chosen for the ceremony; and a letter of summons, which seems to constitute the actual right of appearing at a coronation, was ordered to be drawn up by the Earl of Sunderland. This document, the form of which continues to be followed, runs thus:—

"James R.

"Right trusty and well-beloved cousin, we greet you well. Whereas we have appointed the 23d day of April next for the solemnity of our royal coronation. These are, therefore, to will and command you, all excuses set apart, that you make your personal attendance on us, at the time above mentioned, furnished and appointed, as to your rank and quality appertaineth, there to do and perform such services as shall be required and belonging to you. And whereas we have also resolved, that the coronation of our Royal Consort the Queen shall be solemnized on the same day; we do further require the [Countess] your wife to make her personal attendance on our said Royal Consort, at the time, and in the manner aforesaid: whereof you and she are not to fail. And so we bid you heartily farewell. Given at our Court at Whitehall, the 21st day of March, in the first year of our reign, 1684-5."

In the "Explanation of the Sacred and Royal Habits, and other Ornaments, wherewith the King was invested," Sandford mentions a tablet which hung to the royal chair, and on which were "written, in the Old English letter, these verses"—

> Si quid habent veri vel chronica cana fidesve,
> Clauditur hac cathedra nobilis ecce lapis,
> Ad caput eximus Jacob quondam patriarcha
> Quem posuit cernens numina mira poli:
> Quem tulit ex Scotis spolians quasi victor honoristhan
> Edwardus Primus, Mars velut armipotens,
> Scotorum domitor, notis validissimus Hector,

Anglorum decus, et gloria militiæ.

This must, therefore, have been destroyed since King James's coronation, for it is now lost. There is but one objection to ascribing the verses, with Mr. Taylor, to Edward the First's reign—would he have written "Edwardus *Primus*?"

The queen's crown of state, or that worn on her return from Westminster Hall, seems to have been the most valuable part of the regalia of that day. It is regularly set forth, in its component pearls and diamonds, as of "value 111,900*l.*" (an immense sum at that period), and weighing only eighteen ounces ten pennyweights.

King James and his Queen slept at St. James's Palace on the vigil of St. George, "for the greater convenience of performing their devotions," &c.; and joined the peers and other dignitaries at the Palace of Westminster, by "half an hour after ten." Here the latter were marshalled according to their respective classes, *four* in a rank; placing the youngest on the left, pursuant to what had been before resolved on by his majesty in council, for "the greater glory of the solemnity:" and "note," says our accurate chronicler, "that at *all* former coronations the classes proceeded only by two abreast." The king and queen entered Westminster Hall at half past eleven o'clock precisely; when the dean of Westminster "having, early in the morning, with the assistance of the prebendaries, consecrated the holy oil for their majesties' anointing," (in what manner we are not informed), presented the regalia to the king. Then the queen's regalia were placed before her; and the several noblemen and gentlemen who were to bear the different symbols of royalty to the Abbey were summoned to receive them; the whole procession being ready to move forward exactly at *noon*.

Now came the stately pomp of England's royalty and nobility "through the New Palace Yard into King Street, and so through the Great Sanctuary unto the west door of the collegiate church of St. Peter," as depicted by Sandford in "nineteen sculptures following," or, as modern book-manufacturers would say, in thirty-eight well-executed folio plates, which give the exact appearance of "each degree and order of person in the same," and really form an admirable memorial of such a procession.

The twelve principal ceremonies assigned by this writer to the Abbey are the same in substance with the modern observances. It is noticed by Mr. Taylor that Sandford is the author who *first* terms the presentation of the monarch to the people, and their reply, "the recognition."

The king sat down in St. Edward's chair; and the archbishop, assisted by the dean of Westminster, "reverently put the crown on the king's head" at three of the clock precisely. The queen, having been first anointed on her head and breast, was now crowned and enthroned, and the procession returned to the Hall at "five of the clock."

The first course of the "ambigue" appears to have consisted of "ninety-nine dishes of the most excellent and choicest of all sorts of cold meats, both flesh and fish, excellently well dressed, and ordered all manner of ways;" and the whole feast of 1445 dishes, of the placing of which we have a numbered scheme (a folio plate), and catalogues corresponding. Could this *provoking* volume present its viands to some of our other senses in equal perfection with that in which "the first course of hot meat served up to their majesties' table" meets the eye, it were more reasonable to detain the reader over this part of the work; but, at the late hour of the morning at which we write this, it is too much to dwell on the "cocks' combs," and "petty-toes" and "turkeys-à-la-royale," and "partridges by the dozen," with which it abounds.

The appearance of the champion and the challenge were exactly according to modern usage.

Sandford concludes with an abstract of the record of the Court of Claims, giving both those which were admitted and those which were rejected. The following is a form of judgment respecting the office of lord great chamberlain:—

"Quarum quidem petitionum consideratione maturâ habitâ, eo quod idem Comes de Lyndsey modo existit in possessione et executione officii prædicti, et quod Robertus non ita pridem Carolum Primum fælicissimæ memoriæ, tunc Regem Angliæ, de advisamento Dominorum in Parliamento; quod quidem officium Montague nuper Comes Lyndsey pater ejus, cujus hæres ipse est executus est in coronatione Caroli Secundi nuper Regis Angliæ. Ideo consideratum est per commissionarios prædictos quod clameum prædicti Comitis de Lyndsey ad officium prædictum eidem Comiti de Lyndsey allocetur, exercendum prædicto die Coronationis; et quod clameum prædicti Comitis Derbiæ non allocetur; sed quoad feoda et vadia per dictum Comitem de Lyndsey clamata, clameum ejus quoad poculum de Assay non allocatur, eo quod non constabat prædictis commissionariis Magnum Angliæ Camerarium dictum poculum aliquâ precedenti coronatione habuisse. Sed quod alia clamea prædicta eidem Comiti de Lyndsey allocantur.

"Et postea et ante coronationem prædietam dicta quadraginta Virgatæ Velveti eidem Comiti deliberatæ fuere: et pro reliquis feodis prædictis compositio facta est cum prædicto Comiti, pro ducentis libris sterlingorum, et prædictus Comes de Lyndsey officium Magni Camerarii Angliæ in die Coronationis adimplevit."

And thus the reader has a summary of the contents of this important work.

James II. boasts, in his Memoirs, of having saved the country 60,000*l.* by the omission (for the first time) of the royal procession through the city, at his coronation.

The coronation of William and Mary presented the singular feature of a joint sovereignty over these realms, conferred by public consent. The only alteration this made in the ceremonial was, that another symbol of sovereign power, the orb, was required, and presented in due form to the queen as well as to the king. The new-modelling of the coronation oath, at this period, we have before noticed [109].

It is certainly remarkable that neither of our married queens regnant, Mary or Anne, should have obtained the coronation of their husbands: in neither case was conjugal influence wanted; but the superior force of the people's jealousy of foreign sway was, perhaps, wisely deferred to: in neither reign were other subjects of strife wanted between the crown and the people.

The princes of the illustrious House now seated on the throne have affected no novelties in their coronation ceremonies—except, perhaps, that they have endeavoured to simplify and abridge them. George I. ascended the throne at the age of fifty-five, and was crowned at Westminster, on the 20th of October, 1714. His consort, the Princess Sophia Dorothy of Zell, having fallen under his displeasure for alleged infidelity to her marriage vows, and having been, it is said, divorced from him by the Hanoverian law, was never brought into this country; and never, therefore, acknowledged Queen of England. George II. was crowned with his consort, at Westminster, on the 11th day of October, 1727.

Our late beloved monarch had the happiness of exhibiting to his people the splendid spectacles of his marriage and coronation within the same month of September, 1761. On the 8th of July, in that year, the king first announced to the privy council his intention of demanding in marriage the Princess Charlotte of Mecklenberg, sister of the reigning Duke Adolphus IV., and on the same day signed a proclamation for the assembling of the Court of Claims, and for his own coronation. The queen, being detained by contrary winds, did not arrive in this country until the 6th of September; on the 8th the nuptial ceremony was performed; on the 11th a second proclamation directed that her majesty should be united with her royal consort in the pending coronation ceremonies. These so far varied from that august ceremonial which has recently occupied the public attention, as the presence of a queen consort in the procession to the Abbey, and at the royal feast; her personal attendants; and the body of the peeresses, may be thought to give additional interest and splendour to the scene. The queen entered Westminster Hall the same hour as his majesty, and occupied a chair of state at his left hand, while the regalia were presented by the Dean of Westminster and his attendants. In the procession to the Abbey her majesty's vice-chamberlain took his place immediately following the gentlemen who personated the Dukes of Aquitaine and Normandy, and was succeeded by the other part of the queen's state in the following order:—

The Queen's Vice-Chamberlain, (Lord Viscount Cantalupe,)

Two Gentlemen Ushers.

The Ivory Rod with the Dove, borne by the Earl of Northampton in his robes of estate.	The Queen's Lord Chamberlain, (Duke of Manchester,) in his robes, with his coronet and staff in his hands.	The Sceptre with the Cross, borne by the Duke of Rutland, in his robes of estate.
Two Serjeants at Arms, with their gilt collars and maces. {	The Queen's Crown, borne by the Duke of Bolton, in his robes of estate. }	Two Serjeants Arms, with their gilt collars and maces.

	A Baron of the Cinque-Ports, supporting the Canopy.	Dr. Thomas Hayter, Lord Bishop of Norwich, in his Rochet, supporter to the Queen.		Dr. John Thomas, Lord Bishop of Lincoln, in his Rochet, supporter to the Queen.	A Baron of the Cinque-Ports, supporting the Canopy.
	A Baron, do.				A Baron, do.
	A Baron, do.		the queen, in her Royal Robes of Crimson Velvet; on her head a circlet of Gold, adorned with Jewels; going under a Canopy of Cloth of Gold: her Train borne by Her Royal Highness the Princess Augusta, in her Robes of Estate, assisted by Six Earls' daughters.		A Baron, do.
	A Baron, do.				A Baron, do.
	A Baron, do.				A Baron, do.
	A Baron, do.				A Baron, do.
	A Baron, do.				A Baron, do.
Gentlemen Pensioners, carrying their gilt Axes.	A Baron of the Cinque-Ports, supporting the Canopy.				A Baron of the Cinque-Ports, supporting the Canopy.	*Gentlemen Pensioners, carrying their gilt Axes.*

Lady Jane Steuart.
Lady Elizabeth Montague.
Lady Mary Grey.

Ldy. Mary Douglas
Lady Heneage Finch.
L. Selina Hastings

the princess augusta,
her coronet borne by the Marquess of Carnarvon.
Duchess of Ancaster, Mistress of the Robes.
Two Women of Her Majesty's Bed-Chamber.

The peeresses preceded their respective lords—each rank of the peerage being classed together; that is, the baronesses preceding the barons, the viscountesses the viscounts, and so forth. In the Abbey the queen first ascended the theatre, and stood opposite her chair until the king was seated. His majesty was then anointed and crowned: when the order for the queen's coronation prescribed as follows:—

The anthem being ended, the Archbishop of Canterbury goes to the altar; and the queen arising from her chair on the south side of the area where she sat during the time the king was anointed and crowned, being supported by two bishops, goes towards the altar, attended by the ladies who bear her train, the ladies of the bedchamber, &c., and kneels before it; when the archbishop, being at the north side of the altar, says the following prayer:—

(*Omnipotens sempiterne Deus.*)

Almighty and everlasting God, the fountain of all goodness, give ear, we beseech thee, to our prayers, and multiply thy blessings upon this thy servant, whom in thy name, with all humble devotion, we consecrate our queen. Defend her always with thy mighty hand, protect her on every side, that she may be able to overcome all her enemies; and that with Sarah and Rebecca, Leah and Rachel, and all other blessed and honourable women, she may multiply and rejoice in the fruit of her womb, to the honour of the kingdom and the good government of thy church, through Christ our Lord, who vouchsafed to be born of a virgin that he might redeem the world, who liveth and reigneth with thee, in unity of the Holy Ghost, world without end.

This being done, the queen arises and goes to the faldstool, between king Edward's chair and the steps of the altar, where the groom of the stole to her majesty, and the ladies of the bedchamber, take off her circle or coronet. Then the queen kneels down, and the archbishop pours the holy oil on the crown of her head, in form of a cross, saying these words: — "In the name of the Father, the Son, and the Holy Ghost, let the anointing of this oil increase thine honour, and the grace of God's Holy Spirit establish thee for ever and ever. Amen." — The ladies then open her apparel for the anointing on the breast, which the archbishop also performs, using the same words. After which, he says this prayer:

(*Omnipotens sempiterne Deus.*)

Almighty and everlasting God, we beseech thee of thy abundant goodness poor out the spirit of thy grace and blessing upon this thy servant queen — —; that as by the imposition of our hands she is this day crowned queen, so she may, by thy sanctification, continue always thy chosen servant, through Christ our Lord.

One of the ladies in attendance (having first dried the place anointed with fine cotton wool) then closes the queen's robes at her breast, and after puts a linen coif upon her head; which being done, the archbishop puts the ring (which he receives from the master of the jewel-house) on the fourth finger of her right hand, saying,

Receive this ring, the seal of a sincere faith, that you may avoid all infection of heresy, and by the power of God compel barbarous nations, and bring them to the knowledge of the truth.

His grace then takes the crown from off the altar, and reverently sets it upon the queen's head, saying,

Receive the crown of glory, honour, and joy; and God, the crown of the faithful, who by our episcopal hands, though most unworthy, hath this day set a crown of pure gold upon thy head, enrich you with wisdom and virtue, that after this life you may meet the everlasting Bridegroom our Lord Jesus Christ, who, with the Father and the Holy Ghost, liveth and reigneth for ever and ever. Amen.

The queen being crowned, all the peeresses put on their coronets; the archbishop then puts the sceptre into her majesty's right hand, and the ivory rod into her left, and says the following prayer:

(*Omnium Domine, fons bonorum.*)

O Lord, the fountain of all good things, and the giver of all perfection, grant unto this thy servant — — — our queen, that she may order aright the high dignity she hath obtained, and with good works establish the glory thou hast given her, through Christ our Lord. Amen.

The queen being thus anointed and crowned, and having received all her royal ornaments, the choirs sing an anthem, commonly from Psalm xlv. ver. 1, "My heart is inditing of a good matter," &c. As soon as this is begun, the queen rises from her faldstool, and, being supported by the two bishops, and attended as before, goes up to the theatre: as she approaches the king, she bows herself reverently to his majesty sitting upon his throne; and so is conducted to her own throne on the left hand of the king, where she reposes till the anthem is ended.

The dignity of the monarch, as well as his humility on this august occasion, have been celebrated by the late Bishop Newton. "The king's whole behaviour at the coronation," he says, "was justly admired and commended by every one, and particularly his manner of seating himself on the throne after his coronation. No actor in the character of Pyrrhus, in the Distressed Mother,— not even Booth himself, who was celebrated for it in the Spectator [110],—ever ascended the throne with so much grace and dignity.

There was another particular which those only could observe who sat near the Communion-Table, as did the prebendaries of Westminster. When the king approached the communion-table, in order to receive the sacrament, he inquired of the archbishop, Whether he should not lay aside his crown? The archbishop asked the Bishop of Rochester, but neither of them knew, nor could say, what had been the usual form. The king determined within himself that humility best became such a solemn act of devotion, and took off the crown, and laid it aside during the administration."

That one of the last of the unfortunate race of the Stuarts, Prince Charles, was in London, if not present at the coronation feast, on this occasion, seems to be a fact pretty well established. The Gentleman's Magazine, 1764, (p. 28,) speaks of it as "publicly said, That the young Pretender himself came from Flanders to see the coronation; that he was in Westminster Hall (?) during the ceremony, and in London two or three days before and after it, under the name of Mr. Brown." And Mr. Hume thus writes to one of his literary friends:—"What will surprise you more, Lord Marshal, a few days after the coronation of the present king, told me, that he believed the young Pretender was at that time in London, or, at least, had been so very lately, and had come over to see the show of the coronation, and had actually seen it. I asked my lord the reason for this strange fact. 'Why,' says he, 'a gentleman told me so who saw him there, and whispered in his ear—'Your royal highness is the last of all mortals whom I should expect to see here.'—'It was curiosity that led me,' said the other: 'but I assure you,' added he, 'that the person who is the cause of all this pomp and magnificence, is the man I envy the least.'" A report recently found its way to the public papers, which we have not been able to trace to any authentic source, that a glove was actually thrown from an upper seat in the Hall, as a gage to the king's champion, at this period: that the champion receiving it from his attendants, asked, 'who was his fair foe?' and that the rumour of the day soon connected it with the appearance, and attributed it to the romantic dispositions of the young Chevalier.

Of the late coronation we shall at once consult the best feelings of our own mind, and of the community, by presenting the most copious account we have been able to collect: —

Coronation of his most excellent Majesty King George IV.,

On Thursday the 19th day of July, 1821.

Arrangement fort he Assembling of the Peers and Officers

They were to assemble in the House of Lords	{	Their R. H. the Dukes of the Blood Royal, in their robes of estate, having their coronets, and the Field Marshals their batons, in their hands. The Peers in their robes of estate, having their coronets in their hands. His R. H. Prince Leopold, in the full habit of the Order of the Garter, having his cap and feathers in his hand. The Archbishops and Bishops, vested in their rochets, having their square caps in their hands.
In his place near the Bar	{	The Gentleman Usher of the Black Rod.
In the space below the Bar of the House of Lords	{	The Train-bearers of the Princes of the Blood Royal.
In the space below the Bar of the House of Lords	{	The Attendants on the Lord High Steward, on the Lord Chancellor, the Lord High Constable, and on the Lord Chamberlain of the Household. The Gentlemen Ushers of the White and Green Rods, all in their proper habits.
In the Painted Chamber and adjacent rooms, near the House of Lords	{	The Lord Chief Justice of the King's Bench. The Master of the Rolls. The Vice-Chancellor. The Lord Chief Justice of the Common

                                                Pleas.
The Lord Chief Baron.
The Barons of the Exchequer, and Justices of both Benches.
The Gentlemen of the Privy Chamber.
The Attorney and Solicitor General.
Serjeants at Law.
Masters in Chancery.
The Lord Mayor, Aldermen, Recorder, & Sheriffs of London.
King's Chaplains, having dignities.
Six Clerks in Chancery.

In the Chamber formerly the House of Lords { The Knights Grand Crosses of the Order of the Bath, in the full habit of the Order, wearing their collars; their caps and feathers in their hands.

In the Chamber formerly the House of Lords { The Knights Commanders of the said Order, in their full habits; their caps and feathers in their hands.
The Officers of the said Order, in their mantles, chains, and badges.

In the Chamber formerly called the Prince's Chamber or Robing Room, near the former House of Lords { The Treasurer and Comptroller of the Household.
The Vice-Chamberlain.
The Marquis of Londonderry, in the full habit of the Garter, having his cap and feathers in his hand.
The Register of the said Order, in his mantle, with his book.
Privy Councillors, not being Peers or Knights Grand Crosses of the Bath.
Clerks of the Council in Ordinary.

In his Majesty's Robing, Chamber near the south entrance into Westminster Hall. { The Train-bearers of his Majesty.
Master of the Robes.
Groom of the Robes.

In the room of Chairman of Committees, adjoining the House of Lords {	Lords and Grooms of the Bedchamber. Keeper of the Privy Purse. Equerries and Pages of Honour. Gentlemen Ushers & Aides-de-Camp.
In the Witness-room, adjoining the House of Lords {	Physicians, Surgeons, and Apothecaries.
In the House of Commons and the Lobbies {	Officers of the Band of Gentlemen Pensioners, with their Corps, and the Serjeants at Arms. The Officers of the Yeomen of the Guard, with their Corps.
In the Lobby between the House of Lords and the the Painted Chamber {	The Kings, Heralds, and Pursuivants of Arms.
In Westminster Hall, at the lower end, near the great north door {	Sixteen Barons of the Cinque Ports.
In Westminster Hall, near the north door {	The Knight Marshall and his two Officers.
In Westminster Hall, at the lower end {	His Majesty's Band.
Without the north door of Westminster Hall {	All who are to precede the Knight Marshal in the procession.

His Majesty was, during these preliminary arrangements, in his chamber, near the south entrance into Westminster Hall.

The peers were then called over in the House of Lords by deputy Garter; and proceeded to the Hall, where the other persons appointed to walk in the procession had been previously marshalled on the right and left by the officers of arms; leaving an open passage in the middle, so that the procession with the regalia might pass uninterruptedly up the Hall.

His Majesty, preceded by the great officers of state, entered the Hall a few minutes after ten, and took his seat in the chair of state at the table, when a gun was fired. The deputy lord great chamberlain, the lord high constable, and the deputy earl marshal, ascended the steps, and placed themselves at the outer side of the table.

The lord high steward, the great officers, deputy Garter, and black rod, arranged themselves near the chair of state; the royal train-bearers on each side of the throne.

The lord chamberlain, assisted by officers of the Jewel-office, then brought the sword of state to the lord high constable, who delivered it to the deputy lord great chamberlain, by whom it was laid upon the table; then Curtana, or the sword of mercy, with the two swords of justice, being in like manner presented, were drawn from their scabbards by the deputy lord great chamberlain, and laid on the table before his Majesty; after which the gold spurs were delivered, and also placed on the table. Immediately after, a procession, consisting of the dean and prebendaries of Westminster, in their surplices and rich copes, proceeded up the Hall, from the lower end thereof, in manner following: —

Procession with, and Delivery of, the Regalia.

Serjeant of the Vestry, in a scarlet mantle.

Children of the King's Chapel, in scarlet mantles, four abreast.

Children of the Choir of Westminster, in surplices, four abreast.

Gentlemen of the King's Chapel, in scarlet mantles, four abreast.

Choir of Westminster, in surplices, four abreast.

Sub-Dean of the Chapel Royal.

Two Pursuivants of Arms.

Two Heralds.

The two provincial Kings of Arms.

The Dean of Westminster, carrying St. Edward's Crown on a cushion of cloth of gold.

First Prebendary of Westminster, carrying the Orb.

Second Prebendary, carrying the Sceptre with the Dove.

Third Prebendary, carrying the Sceptre with the Cross.

Fourth Prebendary, carrying St. Edward's Staff.

Fifth Prebendary, carrying the Chalice and Patina.

Sixth Prebendary, carrying the Bible.

In this procession they made their reverences, first at the lower end of the Hall, secondly about the middle, where both the Choirs opening to the right and left a passage, through which the officers of arms passing opened likewise on each side, the seniors placing themselves nearest towards the steps: then the dean and prebendaries having come to the front of the steps, made their third reverence. This being done, the dean and prebendaries being come to the foot of the steps, deputy Garter preceding them (he having waited their coming there), ascended the steps, and approaching near the table before the King, made their last reverence. The dean then presented the crown to the lord high constable, who delivered it to the deputy lord great chamberlain, and it was by him placed on the table before the King. The rest of the regalia was severally delivered by each prebendary, on his knee, to the dean, by him to the lord high constable, by him to the deputy lord great chamberlain, and by him laid on the table. The regalia being thus delivered, the prebendaries and dean returned to the middle of the hall. His Majesty having commanded deputy Garter to summon the noblemen and bishops who were to bear the regalia, the deputy lord great chamberlain, then taking up the several swords, sceptres, the orb, and crown, placed them in the hands of those by whom they were to be carried.

  I. St. Edward's staff, by the Marquess of Salisbury.
 II. The spurs, by Lord Calthorpe, as deputy to the Baroness Grey de Ruthyn.
  III. The sceptre with the cross, by the Marquess Wellesley.
 IV. The pointed sword of temporal justice, by the Earl of Galloway.
 V. The pointed sword of spiritual justice, by the Duke of Northumberland.
  VI. Curtana, or sword of mercy, by the Duke of Newcastle.
   VII. The sword of state, by the Duke of Dorset.
  VIII. The sceptre with the dove, by the Duke of Rutland.
    IX. The orb, by the Duke of Devonshire.
X. St. Edward's crown, by the Marquess of Anglesey, as lord high steward.
   XI. The patina, by the Bishop of Gloucester.
   XII. The chalice, by the Bishop of Chester.
    XIII. The Bible, by the Bishop of Ely.

The two bishops who are to support his Majesty were then summoned by deputy Garter, and, ascending the steps, placed themselves on each side of the king.

Procession to the Abbey.

The second gun was then fired, and the procession moved upon the blue cloth spread on the platform from the throne in Westminster Hall to the great steps in the Abbey church; the following anthem, "O Lord, grant the king a long life," &c. being sung in parts, in succession, with his Majesty's band playing, the sounding of trumpets, and the beating of drums, until the arrival in the Abbey.

Order.

The King's Herb-woman with her six Maids, strewing the way with herbs.

Messenger of the College of Arms, in a scarlet cloak, with the arms of the College embroidered on the left shoulder.

The Dean's Beadle of Westminster, with his staff.

The High Constable of Westminster, with his staff, in a scarlet cloak.

Two Household Fifes with banners of velvet fringed with gold, and five Household Drummers in royal livery, drum-covers of crimson velvet, laced and fringed with gold.

The Drum-Major, in a rich livery, and a crimson scarf fringed with gold.

Eight Trumpets in rich liveries: banners of crimson damask embroidered and fringed with gold, to the silver trumpets.

Kettle-Drums, drum-covers of crimson damask, embroidered and fringed with gold.

Eight Trumpets in liveries, as before.

Serjeant Trumpeter, with his mace.

The Knight Marshal, attended by his Officers.

The Six Clerks in Chancery.

The King's Chaplains having dignities.

The Sheriffs of London.

The Aldermen and Recorder of London.

Masters in Chancery.

The King's Serjeants at Law.

The King's Ancient Serjeant.

The King's Solicitor Gen.   The King's Attorney Gen.

Gentlemen of the Privy Chamber.

Serj. of the Vestry of the Chapel Royal. Serj. Porter.

Children of the Choir of Westminster, in surplices.

Children of the Chapel Royal, in surplices, with scarlet mantles over them.

Choir of Westminster, in surplices.

Gentlemen of the Chapel Royal, in scarlet mantles.

Sub-Dean of the Chapel Royal, in a scarlet gown.

Prebendaries of Westminster, in surplices and rich copes.

The Dean of Westminster, in a surplice and rich cope.

Pursuivants of Scotland and Ireland, in their tabards.

His Majesty's Band.

Officers attendant on the Knights Commanders of the Bath, in their mantles, chains and badges.

Knights Grand Crosses of the Bath (not Peers), in the full habit of their order, caps in their hands.

A Pursuivant of Arms, in his tabard.

Barons of the Exchequer and Justices of both benches.

The Lord Chief Baron of the Exchequer.	The Lord Chief Justice of the Common Pleas.
The Vice Chancellor.	The Master of the Rolls.

The Lord Chief Justice of the King's Bench.

The Clerks of the Council in Ordinary.

Privy Counsellors, not Peers.

Register of the Order of the Garter.

Knights of the Garter (not Peers), in the full habit and collar of the order, caps in their hands.

His Majesty's Vice Chamberlain.

Comptroller of His Majesty's Household.	Treasurer of His Majesty's Household, bearing the crimson bag with the medals.

A Pursuivant of Arms, in his tabard.

Heralds of Scotland and Ireland, in their tabards and collars of SS.

The Standard of Hanover, borne by the Earl of Mayo.

Barons, in their robes of estate, their coronets in their hands.

A Herald, in his tabard and collar of SS.

| The Standard of Ireland, borne by Lord Beresford. | The Standard of Scotland, borne by the Earl of Lauderdale. |

The Bishops of England and Ireland, in their rochets, with their caps in their hands.

Two Heralds, in their tabards and collars of SS.

Viscounts, in their robes of estate, their coronets in their hands.

Two Heralds, in their tabards and collars of SS.

The Standard of England, borne by Lord Hill.

Earls, in their robes of estate, their coronets in their hand.

Two Heralds, in their tabards and collars of SS.

The Union Standard, borne by Earl Harcourt.

Marquesses, in their robes of estate, their coronets in their hands.

The Lord Chamberlain of His Majesty's Household, in his robes of estate, his coronet in his hand, attended by an officer of the Jewel-Office in a scarlet mantle, with a crown embroidered on his left shoulder, bearing a cushion, on which are placed the ruby ring and the sword to be girt about the King.

The Lord Steward of His Majesty's Household, in his robes of estate, his coronet in his hand.

The Royal Standard, borne by the Earl of Harrington.

King of Arms of the Order of St. Michael and St. George, in his tabard, crown in his hand.	Gloucester King of Arms, in his tabard, crown in his hand.	Hanover King of Arms in his tabard, crown in his hand.

Dukes, in their robes of estate, their coronets in their hands.

Ulster King of Arms, in his tabard, crown in his hand.	Clarenceux King of Arms, in his tabard, crown in his hand.	Norroy King of Arms, in his tabard, crown in his hand.

The Lord Privy Seal, in his robes of estate, coronet in his hand.	The Lord President of the Council, in his robes of estate, coronet in his hand.

Archbishops of Ireland.

The Archbishop of York, in his rochet, cap in his hand.

The Lord High Chancellor, in his robes of estate, with his coronet in his hand, bearing his purse, and attended by his Pursebearer.

The Lord Archbishop of Canterbury, in his rochet, cap in his hand.

Two Serjeants at Arms.

The Regalia.

St. Edward's Staff, borne by the Marquess of Salisbury.	The Gold Spurs, borne by the Lord Calthorpe.	The Sceptre with the Cross, borne by the Marquess Wellesley.
The third Sword, borne by the Earl of Galloway.	Curtana, borne by the Duke of Newcastle.	The second Sword, borne by the Duke of Northumberland.

Two Serjeants at Arms.

Usher of the Green Rod.   Usher of the White Rod.

The Lord Mayor of London, in his gown, collar, and jewel, bearing the City mace.	The Lord Lyon of Scotland, in his tabard, carrying his crown and sceptre.	Garter Principal King of Arms, in his tabard, bearing his crown and sceptre.	Gentleman Usher of the Black Rod, bearing his rod.

The Deputy Lord Great Chamberlain of England, in his robes of estate, his coronet and his white staff in his hand.

His Royal Highness the Prince Leopold, in the full habit of the Order of the Garter, carrying in his right hand his baton as Field Marshal, and, in his left, his cap and feathers; his train borne by a Page.

His Royal Highness the Duke of Gloucester, in his robes of estate, carrying, in his right hand, his baton as Field Marshal, and in his left his coronet; his train borne by a Page.

His Royal Highness the Duke of Cambridge, in his robes of estate, carrying, in his right hand, his baton as Field

Marshal, and his coronet in his left; and his train borne by a Page.

His Royal Highness the Duke of Sussex, in his robes of estate, with his coronet in his hand, and his train borne by a Page.

His Royal Highness the Duke of Clarence, in his robes of estate, with his coronet in his hand, and his train borne by a Page.

His Royal Highness the Duke of York, in his robes of estate, carrying, in his right hand, his baton as Field Marshal, and his coronet in his left, and his train borne by a Page.

The High Constable of Ireland, in his robes, coronet in his hand, with his staff.	The High Constable of Scotland, in his robes, coronet in his hand, with his staff.

Two Serjeants at Arms.

The Deputy Earl Marshal with his staff.	The Sword of State, borne by the Duke of Dorset.	The Lord High Constable of England, in his robes, his coronet in his hand, with his staff; attended by a Page carrying his baton of Field Marshal.

Two Serjeants at Arms.

A Gentleman carrying the Staff of the Lord High Steward.	The Sceptre with the Dove, carried by the Duke of Rutland.	St Edward's Crown, carried by the Lord High Steward in his robes.	The Orb, carried by the Duke of Devonshire.	A Gentleman carrying the Coronet of the Lord High Steward.

	The Pantina, borne by the Bishop of Gloucester.	The Bible, borne by the Bishop of Ely.	The Chalice, borne by the Bishop of Chester.	

The King.

Twenty Gentlemen Pensioners, with the Standard Bearer.	Supporter: Lord Bishop of Oxford, for the Lord Bishop of Bath and-Wells.	In the Royal Robes, wearing a cap of estate, adorned with jewels, under a canopy of cloth of gold, borne by Sixteen Barons of the Cinque Ports. His Majesty's train borne by Eight Eldest Sons of Peers, assisted by the Master of the Robes, and followed by the Groom of the Robes.	Supporter: Lord Bishop of Lincoln for the Lord Bishop of Durham.	Twenty Gentlemen Pensioners, with the Lieutenant.
Captain of the		Gold Stick of the		Captain of the

the Guard, in his robes of estate; coronet in his hand.	Waiting, in his robes; coronet in his hand.	Gentlemen Pensioners, in his robes of estate; coronet in his hand.

Lords of the Bedchamber.

The Keeper of His Majesty's Privy Purse.

Grooms of the King's Bedchamber.

Equerries and Pages of Honour.

Aides-de-Camp.

Gentlemen Ushers.

Physicians, Surgeons, Apothecaries.

Ensign of the Yeomen of the Guard.	Lieutenant of the Yeomen of the Guard.

His Majesty's Pages in full State Liveries.

His Majesty's Footmen in full State Liveries.

Exons of the Yeomen of the Guard.	Yeomen of the Guard.	Exons of the Yeomen of the Guard.

Gentleman Harbinger of the Band of Gentlemen Pensioners.

Clerk of the Cheque to the Yeomen of the Guard.	Clerk of the Cheque to the Gentlemen Pensioners.

Yeomen of the Guard, to close the Procession.

On the arrival of the procession at the Abbey, the Herb-woman and her Maids, and the Serjeant-Porter, remained at the entrance within the great west door.

Entrance into Westminster Abbey.

The King entered the west door of the Abbey church at eleven o'clock, and was received with the undermentioned anthem, which was sung by the choir of Westminster, who, with the dean and prebendaries, quitted the procession a little before, and went to the left side of the middle aisle, and remained there till his Majesty arrived, and then followed in the procession next to the regalia.

Anthem I.

Psalm cxxii. verses 1, 5, 6, 7. "I was glad when they said unto me, we will go into the House of the Lord. For there is the seat of judgment, even the seat of the House of David. O pray for the peace of Jerusalem; they shall prosper that love thee. Peace be within thy walls, and plenteousness within thy palaces."

Glory be to the Father, and to the Son, and to the Holy Ghost.

As it was in the beginning, is now, and ever shall be, world without end. Amen.

During the above his Majesty passed through the body of the church, and through the choir up the stairs to the theatre. He then passed his throne and made his humble adoration, and afterwards knelt at the faldstool set for him before his chair; at the same time his Majesty used some short private prayer: he then sat down (not on his throne, but in his chair before and below his throne) and reposed himself.

The Recognition.

When the King was thus placed, the archbishop turned to the east part of the theatre; then, together with the lord chancellor, lord great chamberlain, lord high constable, and earl marshal (Garter king at arms preceding them), went to the other three sides of the theatre, in the order, south, west, and north, and at each side addressed the people in a loud voice; the King at the same time standing up by his chair, turned and showed himself to the people at each of the four sides of the theatre, while the archbishop spoke as follows:—

"Sirs,

"I here present unto you King George the Fourth, the undoubted king of this realm: wherefore all you that come this day to do your homage, are ye willing to do the same?"

This was answered by the loud and repeated acclamations of the persons present, expressive of their willingness and joy, at the same time they cried out—

"God save King George the Fourth!"

Then the trumpets sounded.

The first Oblation.

The archbishop in the meantime went to the altar and put on his cope, and placed himself at the north side of the altar; as did also the bishops who took part in the office.

The officers of the wardrobe, &c. here spread carpets and cushions on the floor and steps of the altar.

And here, first the Bible, paten, and cup, were brought and placed upon the altar. The King then, supported by the two bishops of Durham and Bath, and attended by the dean of Westminster, the lords carrying the regalia before him, went down to the altar, and knelt upon the steps of it, and made his first oblation, uncovered.

Here the pall, or altar-cloth of gold, was delivered by the master of the great wardrobe to the lord great chamberlain, and by him, kneeling, it was presented to his Majesty. The treasurer of the household then delivered a wedge of gold of a pound weight to the lord great chamberlain, which he, kneeling, delivered to his Majesty. The King then (uncovered) delivered them to the archbishop.

The archbishop received them one after another (standing) from his Majesty, and laid the pall reverently upon the altar. The gold was received into the basin; and, with like reverence, was placed upon the altar.

Then the archbishop said the following prayer, the King still kneeling: —

O God, who dwellest in the high and holy place, with them also who are of an humble spirit; mercifully look down upon this thy humble servant, George our King, here humbling himself before thee at thy footstool, and graciously receive these oblations which, in humble acknowledgment of thy sovereignty over all, and of thy great bounty to him in particular, he hath now offered up unto thee, through Jesus Christ, our only Mediator and Advocate. Amen.

When the King had thus offered his oblation, he went to his chair set for him on the south side of the altar, and knelt at his faldstool, and the Litany commenced, which was read by two bishops, vested in copes, and kneeling at a faldstool above the steps of the theatre, on the middle of the east side; the choir read the responses.

In the meantime the lords who carried the regalia, except those who bore the swords, approached the altar, and each presented what he carried to the archbishop, who delivered them to the dean of Westminster, who placed them on the altar. They then retired to the places and seats appointed for them.

The bishops, and the people with them, then said the Lord's Prayer.

The Communion service was read; the people, kneeling,

made the responses to the ten commandments, which were delivered by the archbishop.

Then the archbishop, standing as before, said the following Collect for the King: —

Let us pray.

Almighty God, whose kingdom is everlasting and power infinite: have mercy upon the whole church, and so rule the heart of thy chosen servant George our king and governor, that he (knowing whose minister he is) may above all things seek thy honour and glory; and that we and all his subjects (duly considering whose authority he hath) may faithfully serve, honour, and humbly obey him, in thee and for thee, according to thy blessed word and ordinance, through Jesus Christ our Lord, who with thee and the Holy Ghost, liveth and reigneth ever one God, world without end. Amen.

The following epistle was then read by one of the bishops: —

1 Pet. ii. 13.

Submit yourselves to man for the Lord's sake: whether it be to the king as supreme; or unto governors, as unto them that are sent by him for the punishment of evil-doers, and for the praise of them that do well. For so is the will of God, that with well doing, ye may put to silence the ignorance of foolish men: as free, and not using your liberty for a cloke of maliciousness, but as the servants of God. Honour all men. Love the brotherhood. Fear God. Honour the king.

The Gospel was then read by another bishop, the King and the people standing.

St. Matth. xxii. 15.

Then went the Pharisees, and took counsel how they might entangle him in his talk. And they sent out unto him their disciples, with the Herodians, saying, Master, we know that thou art true, and teachest the way of God in truth, neither carest thou for any man, for thou regardest not the person of men: tell us therefore, What thinkest thou? Is it lawful to give tribute unto Cæsar, or not? But Jesus perceived their wickedness, and said, Why tempt ye me, ye hypocrites? Show me the tribute money. And they brought unto him a penny. And he saith unto them, Whose is this image and superscription? They say unto him, Cæsar's. Then saith he unto them, Render therefore unto Cæsar, the things which are Cæsar's: and unto God, the things that are God's. When they had heard these words, they marvelled, and left him, and went their way.

Then the Archbishop read the Nicene Creed; the King and the people standing as before.

I believe in one God the Father, &c. &c.

At the end of the Creed, the archbishop of York preached the sermon in the pulpit placed against the pillar at the north-east corner of the theatre. The King listened to the same sitting in his chair on the south side of the altar, over against the pulpit.

The Sermon.

His text was the 23d chapter of the Second Book of Samuel, and the 3d and 4th verses.

"He that ruleth over men must be just, ruling in the fear of God. And he shall be as the light of the morning, when the sun riseth, even a morning without clouds."

Such, observed his Grace, were the words of a pious Prince, whose opinions had been matured by experience. A steady adherence to the maxims there laid down could scarcely fail to preserve from error, and would at once inspire the subject with a reverence for the sovereign, and impress the sovereign with a sense of those obligations which bound him to render justice to the people. The duties of kings were of a particular nature, and the subject was one of more than common importance upon a day like the present, which was to be marked by the solemnization of that contract by which the king bound himself to rule with justice and equity. The highest station, and the most exalted rank, were not free from the infirmities of nature; and it therefore behoved the sovereign not to forget that he was himself but the minister of a higher authority, and that it was his duty so to exert the power which resided in him, as to secure the love and attachment of his people. The history of all nations would show that the people were not ungrateful under the administration of good kings. It was true, that it was the disposition of human nature to imagine grievances where in reality none existed; but still there were many real grievances which a king had the power and ought to have the disposition to relieve. The text which he had just read naturally led to the consideration of what were the principles which constituted a good government. In a moral point of view, no distinction could be drawn between the duties due from one individual to another, and those due from a monarch to his people. It ought not to be forgotten that natural equity demanded the same degree of observance with regard to the contract entered into with a whole people, as it did to those obligations into which individuals entered with regard to each other. There was no higher duty incumbent upon kings than that of selecting proper persons to represent them in the different departments of state. Upon that step how much of the happiness of the people would depend! It was a proud reflection, that no nation stood more high in the estimation of surrounding nations, or was more admired for its morality, its attention to religious duties, the justice of its measures, or the soundness of its general policy, than our own. He insisted that it was necessary to preserve and to encourage that feeling by a reciprocal attention, on the parts both of the monarch and of the people, to those duties which were due from each. If such an attention was not given, it would be in vain to expect national happiness; and however successful we might be in our dealings with foreign nations, still it ought not to be forgotten that the apparent prosperity of a nation ought not to be regarded as an evidence of the happiness of its people. But, above all, it was necessary that the king should seek to secure respect to himself and obedience to the laws, by displaying in his own person an example of good conduct. It was the province of the monarch to reflect that he was responsible not only for his own actions, but also for that evil which the direct influence of his own example might accomplish. Well, therefore, had it been said in the words of his text, "He that ruleth over men must be just, ruling in the fear of God." A good government would secure to itself a due observance of its own rights, and would also afford to the people the protection of its wisdom and power. His Grace, after some general remarks on the duties of kings, proceeded to observe, that the House of Hanover had always been distinguished by its devotion to the interests of true religion. Our late venerable sovereign had presented a striking example of royal goodness by the attention which had always marked both his public and private conduct; and we were bound to hope (upon looking to the past) that the sovereign who was now about to receive the imperial crown of his ancestors would be equally remarkable for the exemplary discharge of the duties of royalty. Nor ought it to be forgotten that the illustrious individual, to whom he had alluded, had not been unused to the functions of government; and that he had given proofs of such capacity and disposition as enabled us to form good hopes of the future. At the time when he had first been called to the exercise of the supreme power, he had found the country involved in a war which threatened its existence—a war which had not been engaged in on our part for the purposes of aggrandisement, but for the defence and preservation of our rights. Under his superintendence that war had been concluded, and its conclusion had been marked by exertions unparalleled in the history of any nation. Under such auspices, therefore, it was right to anticipate all those blessings which could arise on one hand from the protection of a just and wise monarch, and on the other from the affections of a loyal and happy people. "Let us then adore that Almighty Providence which has conferred upon us such a sovereign; let us implore that blessings may be multiplied on his head, and that his reign may be prosperous and happy."

His Grace commenced the Sermon at a quarter past twelve, and ended it at about a quarter to one.

The King was uncovered during the offering and the service that followed; when the sermon commenced he put on his cap of crimson velvet turned up with ermine, and remained covered to the end of it.

On his Majesty's right hand stood the bishop of Durham, and beyond him, on the same side, the lords that carried the swords. On his Majesty's left hand stood the bishop of Bath and Wells, and the lord great chamberlain.

On the north side of the altar sat the archbishop in a purple velvet chair; the bishops were placed on forms along the north side of the wall, betwixt the King and the pulpit. Near the archbishop stood garter, king at arms. On the south side, east of the King's chair, nearer to the altar, stood the dean of Westminster, the rest of the bishops who took part in the church service, and the prebendaries of Westminster.

The Oath.

When the Sermon ended, the archbishop went to the King, and standing before him, (his Majesty, on Thursday, the 27th of April, 1820, in the presence of the two Houses of Parliament, made and signed the declaration against popery,) administered the coronation oath, first asking the King—

Sir; is your Majesty willing to take the oath?

The King answered:—I am willing.

The archbishop then ministered these questions; and the King, having a copy of the printed form and order of the coronation service in his hands, answered each question severally, as follows:—

Arch. Will you solemnly promise and swear to govern the people of this United Kingdom of Great Britain and Ireland, and the dominions thereto belonging, according to the statutes in Parliament agreed on, and the respective laws and customs of the same?

King. I solemnly promise so to do.

Arch. Will you to your power cause law and justice, in mercy, to be executed in all your judgments?

King. I will.

Arch. Will you to the utmost of your power maintain the laws of God, the true profession of the Gospel, and the Protestant Reformed Religion established by law? And will you maintain and preserve inviolably the settlement of the United Church of England and Ireland, and the doctrine, worship, discipline, and government thereof, as by law established within England and Ireland, and the territories thereunto belonging? And will you preserve unto the bishops and clergy of England and Ireland, and to the United Church committed to their charge, all such rights and privileges, as by law do, or shall appertain to them, or any of them?

King. All this I promise to do.

Then the King, arising out of his chair, supported as before, and assisted by the lord great chamberlain, the sword of state being carried before him, went to the altar, and there being uncovered, made his solemn oath in the sight of all the people, to observe the premises; laying his right hand upon the Holy Gospel in the great Bible, which was before carried in the procession, and was now brought from the altar by the archbishop, and tendered to him as he knelt upon the steps, saying these words: —

The things which I have here before promised, I will perform and keep.

So help me God.

Then the King kissed the book, and signed the oath.

The Anointing.

(In the morning early, care was taken that the ampula was filled with oil, and the spoon laid ready upon the altar of the Abbey church.)

The King having thus taken his oath, returned again at the chair; and kneeling at his faldstool, the archbishop begun the hymn Veni, Creator Spiritus, and the choir sang it out.

Anthem II.

> Come, Holy Ghost, our souls inspire,
> And warm them with thy heav'nly fire.
> Thou who th' anointing Spirit art,
> To us thy sevenfold gifts impart.
> Let thy bless'd unction from above
> Be to us comfort, life, and love.
> Enable with celestial light
> The weakness of our mortal sight:
> Anoint our hearts, and cheer our face,
> With the abundance of thy grace:
> Keep far our foes, give peace at home;
> Where thou dost dwell, no ill can come:
> Teach us to know the Father, Son,
> And Spirit of both, to be but one,
> That so, through ages all along,
> This may be our triumphant song;
> In thee, O Lord, we make our boast,
> Father, Son, and Holy Ghost.

This being ended, the archbishop said this prayer: —

O Lord, Holy Father, who by anointing with oil didst of old make and consecrate kings, priests, and prophets, to teach and govern thy people Israel: bless and sanctify thy chosen servant George, who by our office and ministry is now to be anointed with this oil, and consecrated King of this realm: strengthen him, O Lord, with the Holy Ghost the Comforter; Confirm and stablish him with thy free and princely spirit, the spirit of wisdom and government, the spirit of counsel and ghostly strength, the spirit of knowledge and true godliness, and fill him, O Lord, with the spirit of thy holy fear, now and for ever. Amen.

This prayer being ended, the choir sang:

Anthem III.

Zadok the priest, and Nathan the prophet, anointed Solomon King; and all the people rejoiced, and said, God save the King! Long live the King! May the King live for ever! Amen. Hallelujah!

In the meantime the King, rising from his devotions, went before the altar, supported and attended as before.

The King sat down in his chair, placed in the midst of the area over against the altar, with the faldstool before it, wherein he was anointed. Four knights of the garter held over him a rich pall of silk, or cloth of gold; the dean of Westminster took the ampula and spoon from off the altar, poured some of the holy oil into the spoon, and with it the archbishop anointed the King, in the form of a cross:

1. On the crown of the head, saying,

Be thy head anointed with holy oil, as kings, priests, and prophets were anointed.

2. On the breast, saying,

Be thy breast anointed with holy oil.

3. On the palms of both the hands, saying,

Be thy hands anointed with holy oil:

And as Solomon was anointed king by Zadok the priest, and Nathan the prophet, so be you anointed, blessed, and consecrated King over this people, whom the Lord your God hath given you to rule and govern, in the name of the father, and of the Son, and of the Holy Ghost. Amen.

Then the dean of Westminster laid the ampula and spoon upon the altar, and the King kneeling down at the faldstool, and the archbishop standing on the north side of the altar, said this prayer or blessing over him: —

Our Lord Jesus Christ, the Son of God, who by his Father was anointed with the oil of gladness above his fellows, by his holy anointing pour down upon your head and heart the blessing of the Holy Ghost, and prosper the works of your hands: that by the assistance of his heavenly grace you may preserve the people committed to your charge in wealth, peace, and godliness; and after a long and glorious course of ruling this temporal kingdom wisely, justly, and religiously, you may at last be made partaker of an eternal kingdom, through the merits of Jesus Christ our Lord. Amen.

This prayer being ended, the King arose, and sat down again in his chair, and the dean of Westminster wiped and dried all the places anointed, with fine linen, or fine bombast wool, delivered to him by the lord great chamberlain.

The Presenting of the Spurs and Word, and the Girding and Oblation oft he Said Sword.

Then the spurs were brought from the altar by the dean of Westminster, and delivered to a nobleman thereto appointed by the King, who, kneeling down, presents them to His Majesty, who forthwith sent them back to the altar.

Then the lord who carried the sword of state, returned the said sword to the officers of the Jewel-house, which was thereupon deposited in the traverse in King Edward's chapel; he received thence, in lieu thereof, another sword, in a scabbard of purple velvet, provided for the King to be girt withal, which he delivered to the archbishop; and the archbishop, laying it on the altar, said the following prayer:—

Hear our prayers, O Lord, we beseech thee, and so direct and support thy servant King George, who is now to be girt with this sword, that he may not bear it in vain; but may use it as the minister of God, for the terror and punishment of evil-doers, and for the protection and encouragement of those that do well, through Jesus Christ our Lord. Amen.

Then the archbishop took the sword from off the altar, and (the bishops assisting, and going along with him) delivered it into the King's right hand, and he holding it, the archbishop said:—

Receive this kingly sword, brought now from the altar of God, and delivered to you by the hands of us the bishops and servants of God, though unworthy.

The King stood up, the sword was girt about him by the lord great chamberlain, and then, the King sitting down, the archbishop said:—

Remember him of whom the royal Psalmist did prophesy, saying, "Gird thee with thy sword upon thy thigh, O thou most mighty, good luck have thou with thine honour, ride on prosperously, because of truth, meekness, and righteousness;" and be thou a follower of him. With this sword do justice, stop the growth of iniquity, protect the holy Church of God, help and defend widows and orphans, restore the things that are gone to decay, maintain the things that are restored, punish and reform what is amiss, and confirm what is in good order: that doing these things, you may be glorious in all virtue; and so represent our Lord Jesus Christ in this life, that you may reign for ever with him in the life which is to come. Amen.

Then the King, rising up, ungirded his sword, and, going to the altar, offered it there in the scabbard, and then returned and sat down in his chair: and the chief peer offered the price of it, namely, a hundred shillings, and having thus redeemed it, received it from off the altar by the dean of Westminster, and drew it out of the scabbard, and carried it naked before his Majesty during the rest of the solemnity.

The Investing with the Armill & Royal Robe, and the Delivery of the Orb.

Then the King arising, the dean of Westminster took the armill from the master of the great wardrobe, and put it about his Majesty's neck, and tied it to the bowings of his arms, above and below the elbows, with silk strings; the archbishop standing before the King, and saying:—

Receive this armill as a token of the divine mercy embracing you on every side.

Next the robe royal, or purple robe of state, of cloth of tissue, lined or furred with ermines, was by the master of the great wardrobe delivered to the dean of Westminster, and by him put upon the King, standing; the crimson robe which he wore before being first taken off by the lord great chamberlain: the King having received it, sat down, and then the orb with the cross was brought from the altar by the dean of Westminster, and delivered into the King's hand by the archbishop, pronouncing this blessing and exhortation:—

Receive this imperial robe and orb, and the Lord your God endue you with knowledge and wisdom, with majesty and with power from on high; the Lord clothe you with the robe of righteousness, and with the garments of salvation. And when you see this orb set under the cross, remember that the whole world is subject to the power and empire of Christ our Redeemer. For He is the Prince of the kings of the earth; King of kings, and Lord of lords: so that no man can reign happily, who deriveth not his authority from him, and directeth not all his actions according to his laws.

The Investiture per Annulum et Baculum.

Then the master of the Jewel-house delivered the King's ring to the archbishop, in which a table jewel was enchased; the archbishop put it on the fourth finger of his Majesty's right hand, and said:—

Receive this ring, the ensign of kingly dignity, and of defence of the Catholic faith; and as you are this day solemnly invested in the government of this earthly kingdom, so may you be sealed with that spirit of promise, which is the earnest of an heavenly inheritance, and reign with Him who is the blessed and only Potentate, to whom be glory for ever and ever. Amen.

The King delivered his orb to the dean of Westminster, to be by him laid upon the altar; and then the dean of Westminster brought the sceptre and rod to the archbishop; and the lord of the manor of Worksop (who claimed to hold an estate by the service of presenting to the King a right hand glove on the day of his coronation, and supporting the King's right arm whilst he holds the sceptre with the cross) delivered to the King a pair of rich gloves, and in any occasion happening afterwards, supported his Majesty's right arm, or held his sceptre by him.

The gloves being put on, the archbishop delivered the sceptre, with the cross, into the King's right hand, saying,

Receive the royal sceptre, the ensign of kingly power and justice.

And then he delivered the rod, with the dove, into the King's left hand, and said,

Receive the rod of equity and mercy: and God, from whom all holy desires, all good counsels, and all just works do proceed, direct and assist you in the administration and exercise of all those powers he hath given you. Be so merciful, that you be not too remiss; so execute justice, that you forget not mercy. Punish the wicked, protect the oppressed; and the blessing of him who was ready to perish shall be upon you; thus in all things following His great and holy example, of whom the prophet David said, "Thou lovest righteousness, and hatest iniquity; the sceptre of thy kingdom is a right sceptre;" even Jesus Christ our Lord. Amen.

The Putting on of the Crown.

The archbishop, standing before the altar, took the crown into his hands, and laying it again before him upon the altar, said,

O God, who crownest thy faithful servants with mercy and loving-kindness; look down upon this thy servant George our King, who now in lowly devotion boweth his head to thy Divine Majesty; and as thou dost this day set a crown of pure gold upon his head, so enrich his royal heart with thy heavenly grace; and crown him with all princely virtues, which may adorn the high station wherein thou hast placed him, through Jesus Christ our Lord, to whom be honour and glory, for ever and ever. Amen.

Then the King sat down in king Edward's chair; the archbishop, assisted with other bishops, came from the altar; the dean of Westminster brought the crown, and the archbishop taking it of him, reverently put it upon the King's head. At the sight whereof the people, with loud and repeated shouts, cried, "God save the King!" and the trumpets sounded, and, by a signal given, the great guns at the Tower were shot off.

The noise ceasing, the archbishop rose and said,

Be strong and of good courage: observe the commandments of God, and walk in his holy ways: fight the good fight of faith, and lay hold on eternal life; that in this world you may be crowned with success and honour, and when you have finished your course, you may receive a crown of righteousness, which God the righteous Judge shall give you in that day. Amen.

Then the choir sung this short anthem.

Anthem IV.

The King shall rejoice in thy strength, O Lord: exceeding glad shall he be of thy salvation. Thou hast presented him with the blessings of goodness, and hast set a crown of pure gold upon his head. Hallelujah. Amen.

As soon as the King was crowned, the peers, &c. put on their coronets and caps.

The Presenting of the Holy Bible.

The dean of Westminster took the Holy Bible, which was carried in the procession, from off the altar, and delivered it to the archbishop, who, with the rest of the bishops going along with him, presented it to the King, first saying these words to him:—

Our Gracious King; we present unto your Majesty this book, the most valuable thing that this world affordeth. Here is wisdom; this is the royal law; these are the lively oracles of God. Blessed is he that readeth, and they that hear the words of this book; that keep, and do, the things contained in it. For these are the words of eternal life, able to make you wise and happy in this world, nay wise unto salvation, and so happy for evermore, through faith which is in Christ Jesus; to whom be glory for ever. Amen.

Then the King delivered back the Bible to the archbishop, who gave it to the dean of Westminster, to be reverently placed again upon the holy altar.

The Benedicton, and Te Deum.

And now the King having been thus anointed and crowned, and having received all the ensigns of royalty, the archbishop solemnly blessed him, and all the bishops standing about him, with the rest of the peers, with a loud and hearty Amen.

The Lord bless and keep you: the Lord make the light of his countenance to shine for ever upon you, and be gracious unto you: the Lord protect you in all your ways, preserve you from every evil thing, and prosper you in every thing good. Amen.

The Lord give you a faithful senate, wise and upright counsellors and magistrates, a loyal nobility, and a dutiful gentry; a pious and learned and useful clergy; an honest, industrious, and obedient commonalty. Amen.

In your days may mercy and truth meet together, and righteousness and peace kiss each other; may wisdom and knowledge be the stability of your times, and the fear of the Lord your treasure. Amen.

The Lord make your days many, and your reign prosperous; your fleets and armies victorious: and may you be reverenced and beloved by all your subjects, and ever increase in favour with God and man. Amen.

The glorious Majesty of the Lord our God be upon you: may he bless you with all temporal and spiritual happiness in this world, and crown you with glory and immortality in the world to come. Amen.

The Lord give you a religious and victorious posterity to rule these kingdoms in all ages. Amen.

Then the archbishop turned to the people, and said: —

And the same Lord God Almighty grant, that the clergy and nobles assembled here for this great and solemn service, and together with them all the people of the land, fearing God, and honouring the King, may by the merciful superintendency of the Divine Providence, and the vigilant care of our gracious Sovereign, continually enjoy peace, plenty, and prosperity, through Jesus Christ our Lord; to whom, with the Eternal Father, and God the Holy Ghost, be glory in the church world without end. Amen.

The blessing being thus given, the King sat down in his chair, vouchsafed to kiss the archbishop and bishops assisting at his coronation, they kneeling before him one after another.

Then the choir began to sing the Te Deum, and the King went up to the theatre on which the throne is placed, all the bishops, great officers, and other peers, attending him, and then he sat down and reposed himself in his chair, below the throne.

Anthem V.

Te Deum.

We praise thee, O God; we acknowledge thee to be the Lord.

All the earth doth worship thee: the Father everlasting.

To thee all angels cry aloud: the heavens, and all the powers therein.

To thee Cherubin and Seraphin: continually do cry,

Holy, holy, holy: Lord God of Sabaoth.

Heaven and earth are full of the majesty of thy glory.

The glorious company of the Apostles: praise thee.

The goodly fellowship of the Prophets: praise thee.

The noble army of Martyrs: praise thee.

The holy Church throughout all the world: doth acknowledge thee;

The Father: of an infinite Majesty;

Thine honourable, true, and only Son;

Also the Holy Ghost: the Comforter.

Thou art the King of glory: O Christ.

Thou art the everlasting Son: of the Father.

When thou tookest upon thee to deliver man: thou didst not abhor the virgin's womb.

When thou hadst overcome the sharpness of death: thou didst open the kingdom of heaven to all believers.

Thou sittest at the right hand of God: in the glory of the Father.

We believe that thou shalt come: to be our judge.

We therefore pray thee, help thy servants: whom thou hast redeemed with thy precious blood.

Make them to be numbered with thy saints: in glory everlasting.

O Lord save thy people: and bless thine heritage.

Govern them: and lift them up for ever.

Day by day we magnify thee.

And we worship thy name: ever world without end.

Vouchsafe, O Lord: to keep us this day without sin.

O Lord, have mercy upon us: have mercy upon us.

O Lord, let thy mercy lighten upon us: as our trust is in thee.

O Lord, in thee have I trusted: let me never be confounded.

The Inthronization.

The *Te Deum* being ended, the King was lifted up into his throne by the archbishop and bishops, and other peers of the kingdom. And being inthronized or placed therein, all the great officers, those that bore the swords, and the sceptres, and the rest of the nobles, stood round about the steps of the throne, and the archbishop standing before the King, said,

Stand firm, and hold fast, from henceforth, the seat and imperial dignity which is this day delivered unto you in the name, and by the authority of Almighty God, and by the hands of us the bishops and servants of God, though unworthy; and as you see us to approach nearer to God's altar, so vouchsafe the more graciously to continue to us your royal favour and protection. And the Lord God Almighty, whose ministers we are, and the stewards of his mysteries, establish your throne in righteousness, that it may stand fast for evermore, like as the sun before Him, and as the faithful witness in heaven. Amen.

The Homage.

The exhortation being ended, all the peers present did homage publicly and solemnly unto the King upon the theatre, and in the meantime the treasurer of the household threw among the people medals of gold and silver, as the King's princely largess or donative.

The archbishop first knelt down before his Majesty's knees, and the rest of the bishops knelt on either hand, and about him; and they did their homage together, for the shortening of the ceremony, the archbishop saying:

I Charles archbishop of Canterbury [and so every one of the rest, I N. bishop of N. repeating the rest audibly after the archbishop] will be faithful and true, and faith and truth will bear, unto you our Sovereign Lord, and your heirs, kings of the united kingdom of Great Britain and Ireland. And I will do, and truly acknowledge the service of the lands which I claim to hold of you, as in right of the church.

So help me God.

Then the archbishop kissed the King's left cheek, and so the rest of the bishops present after him.

After which the other peers of the realm did their homage in like manner, the dukes first by themselves, and so the marquesses, the earls, the viscounts, and the barons, severally; the first of each order kneeling before his Majesty, and the rest with and about him, all putting off their coronets, and the first of each class beginning, and the last saying after him: —

I N. duke, or earl, &c. of N. do become your liege man of life and limb, and of earthly worship, and faith and truth I will bear unto you, to live and die, against all manner of folks.

So help me God.

The peers having done their homage, they stood all together round about the King; and each class or degree going by themselves, or (as it was at the coronation of King Charles the First and Second) every peer one by one, in order, put off their coronets, singly ascended the throne again, and stretching forth their hands, touched the crown on his Majesty's head, as promising by that ceremony to be ever ready to support it with all their power, and then every one of them kissed the King's cheek.

While the peers were thus doing their homage, and the medals thrown about, the King delivered his sceptre with the cross to the lord of the manor of Worksop, to hold; and the other sceptre, or rod, with the dove, to the lord that carried it in the procession.

And the bishops that supported the King in the procession also eased him, by supporting the crown, as there was occasion.

The Final Anthem.

While the medals were scattered, and the homage of the lords performed, the choir sung this anthem, with instrumental music of all sorts, as a solemn conclusion of the King's coronation.

Anthem VI.

Blessed be thou, Lord God of Israel, our Father, for ever and ever. Thine, O Lord, is the greatness and the power, and the victory, and the majesty; for all that is in the heaven and the earth are thine. Thine is the kingdom, O Lord; and thou art exalted as head over all. Both riches and honour come of thee, and thou reignest over all; and in thine hand is power and might; and in thine hand it is to make great, and to give strength unto all. Now, therefore, our God, we thank thee, and praise thy glorious name.

At the end of this anthem the drums beat, and the trumpets

sounded, and all the people shouted, crying out,

    God save King George the Fourth!

    Long live King George!

    May the King live for ever!

The solemnity of the King's coronation being thus ended, the archbishop left the King in his throne, and went down to the altar.

The Communion.

Then the Offertory began, the archbishop reading these sentences: —

Let your light so shine before men that they may see your good works, and glorify your Father which is in heaven.

Charge them who are rich in this world, that they be ready to give, and glad to distribute; laying up in store for themselves a good foundation against the time to come, that they may attain eternal life.

The King descended from his throne, supported and attended as before; and went to the steps of the altar, and knelt down there.

And first the King offered bread and wine for the Communion, which were brought out of king Edward's chapel, and delivered into his hands, the bread upon the paten by the bishop that read the Epistle, and the wine in the chalice by the bishop that read the Gospel; these were by the archbishop received from the King, and reverently placed upon the altar, and decently covered with a fair linen cloth, the archbishop first saying this prayer: —

Bless, O Lord, we beseech thee, these thy gifts, and sanctify them unto this holy use, that by them we may be made partakers of the body and blood of thine only begotten Son Jesus Christ, and fed unto everlasting life of soul and body: and that thy servant King George may be enabled to the discharge of his weighty office, whereunto of thy great goodness thou hast called and appointed him. Grant this, O Lord, for Jesus Christ's sake, our only Mediator and Advocate. Amen.

Then the King kneeling, as before, made his second Oblation, offering a mark weight of gold, which the treasurer of the household delivered to the lord great chamberlain, and he to His Majesty. And the archbishop came to him, and received it in the basin, and placed it upon the altar. After which the bishop said:—

O God, who dwellest in the high and holy place, with them also who are of an humble spirit; look down mercifully upon this thy servant George, our King, here humbling himself before thee at thy footstool; and graciously receive these oblations, which in humble acknowledgment of thy sovereignty over all, and of thy great bounty to him in particular, he has now offered up unto thee, through Jesus Christ, our only Mediator and Advocate. Amen.

Then the King returned to his chair, and knelt down at his faldstool; the archbishop said:—

Let us pray for the whole state of Christ's church militant here on earth.

Almighty and ever-living God, who by thy holy Apostle hast taught us to make prayers and supplications, and to give thanks for all men: we humbly beseech thee most mercifully to receive these our prayers which we offer unto thy Divine Majesty, beseeching thee to inspire continually the universal church with the spirit of truth, unity, and concord: and grant that all they that do confess thy holy name, may agree in the truth of thy holy word, and live in unity and godly love. We beseech thee also to save and defend all Christian kings, princes, and governors; and especially thy servant George our King, that under him we may be godly and quietly governed: and grant unto his whole council, and to all that are put in authority under him, that they may truly and indifferently minister justice, to the punishment of wickedness and vice, and to the maintenance of thy true religion and virtue. Give grace, O heavenly Father, to all bishops and curates, that they may both by their life and doctrine set forth thy true and lively word, and rightly and duly administer thy holy sacraments: and to all thy people give thy heavenly grace, and especially to this congregation here present, that with meek heart and due reverence they may hear and receive thy holy word, truly serving thee in holiness and righteousness all the days of their life. And we most humbly beseech thee of thy goodness, O Lord, to comfort and succour all them who in this transitory life are in trouble, sorrow, need, sickness, or any other adversity. And we also bless thy holy name, for all thy servants departed this life in thy faith and fear; beseeching thee to give us grace so to follow their good examples, that with them we may be partakers of thy heavenly kingdom. Grant this, O Father, for Jesus Christ's sake, our only Mediator and Advocate. Amen.

The Exhortation.

Ye that do truly and earnestly repent you of your sins, and are in love and charity with your neighbours, and intend to lead a new life, following the commandments of God, and walking from henceforth in his holy ways; draw near with faith, and take this holy Sacrament to your comfort; and make your humble confession to Almighty God, meekly kneeling upon your knees.

The General Confession.

Almighty God, Father of our Lord Jesus Christ, Maker of all things, Judge of all men; we acknowledge and bewail our manifold sins and wickedness, which we from time to time most grievously have committed, by thought, word, and deed, against thy divine Majesty, provoking most justly thy wrath and indignation against us. We do earnestly repent, and are heartily sorry for these our misdoings; the remembrance of them is grievous unto us; the burden of them is intolerable. Have mercy upon us, have mercy upon us, most merciful Father; for thy Son our Lord Jesus Christ's sake, forgive us all that is past, and grant that we may ever hereafter serve and please thee, in newness of life, to the honour and glory of thy name, through Jesus Christ our Lord. Amen.

The Absolution.

Almighty God our heavenly Father, who of his great mercy hath promised forgiveness of sins to all them that with hearty repentance, and true faith, turn unto him; have mercy upon you, pardon and deliver you from all your sins, confirm and strengthen you in all goodness, and bring you to everlasting life, through Jesus Christ our Lord. Amen.

After which was said,

Hear what comfortable words our Saviour saith unto all that truly turn to him.

Come unto me, all that travail and are heavy laden, and I will refresh you. St. Matt. xi. 28.

So God loved the world, that he gave his only begotten Son to the world, and that all that believe in him should not perish, but have everlasting life. St. John, iii. 16.

Hear also what St. Paul saith:

This is a true saying, and worthy of all men to be received, that Christ Jesus came into the world to save sinners. 1 Tim. i. 15.

Hear also what St. John saith:

If any man sin, we have an advocate with the Father, Jesus Christ the righteous, and he is the propitiation for our sins. 1 John, ii. 1.

After which the archbishop proceeded, saying,

Arch. Lift up your hearts.

Answ. We lift them unto the Lord.

Arch. Let us give thanks unto our Lord God.

Answ. It is meet and right so to do.

Then the archbishop turned to the Lord's table, and said,

It is very meet, right, and our bounden duty, that we should at all times, and in all places, give thanks unto thee, O Lord, Holy

Father, Almighty everlasting God:

Who hast at this time given us thy servant our sovereign King George, to be the Defender of the Faith, and the protector of thy people:

Therefore with angels and archangels, and with all the company of heaven, we laud and magnify thy glorious name, evermore praising thee, and saying, Holy, holy, holy, Lord God of hosts, heaven and earth are full of thy glory. Glory be to thee, O Lord most high. Amen.

The Prayer of Address.

We do not presume to come to this thy table, O merciful God, trusting in our own righteousness, but thy manifold great mercies. We are not worthy so much as to gather up the crumbs under thy table. But thou art the same God, whose property is always to have mercy; grant us therefore, gracious God, so to eat the flesh of thy dear Son, Jesus Christ, to drink his blood, that our sinful bodies may be made clean by his body, our souls washed through his most precious blood. That we may evermore dwell with him, and he with us. Amen.

The Prayer of Consecration.

Almighty God, our heavenly Father, who of thy tender mercy didst give thine only Son Jesus Christ to suffer death upon the cross for our redemption, who made there (by his one oblation of himself once offered) a full, perfect, and sufficient sacrifice, oblation, and satisfaction for the sins of the whole world, and did institute, and in his holy Gospel command us to continue a perpetual memory of that his precious death to his coming again; hear us, O merciful Father, we most humbly beseech thee; and grant that we, receiving these thy creatures of bread and wine, according to thy Son our Saviour Jesus Christ's holy institution, in remembrance of his death and passion, may be partakers of his most holy body and blood: who in the same night that he was betrayed took bread [111], and when he had given thanks, he brake it [112], and gave it to his disciples, saying, Take, eat [113], this is my body which is given for you, do this in remembrance of me. Likewise, after supper [114] he took the cup, and when he had given thanks, he gave it to them, saying, Drink ye all of this, for this [115] is my blood of the New Testament, which is shed for you and for many for the remission of sins: do this, as oft as ye shall drink it, in remembrance of me. Amen.

When the archbishop, and dean of Westminster, with the bishops' assistants, namely, the preacher, and those who read the Litany, and the Epistle and Gospel, had communicated in both kinds, the archbishop administered the bread, and the dean of Westminster the cup, to the King.

At the delivery of the bread, was said,

The body of our Lord Jesus Christ, which was given for thee, preserve thy body and soul unto everlasting life. Take and eat this in remembrance that Christ died for thee, and feed on him in thy heart by faith with thanksgiving.

At the delivery of the cup,

The blood of our Lord Jesus Christ, which was shed for thee, preserve thy body and soul unto everlasting life. Drink this in remembrance that Christ's blood was shed for thee, and be thankful.

While the King received, the bishop appointed for that service held a towel of white silk, or fine linen, before him.

Then the archbishop went on to the Post Communion, saying,—

Our Father which art in heaven; hallowed be thy name. Thy kingdom come. Thy will be done in earth, as it is in heaven. Give us this day our daily bread; and forgive us our trespasses as we forgive them who trespass against us. Lead us not into temptation, but deliver us from evil; for thine is the kingdom, and the power, and the glory, for ever. Amen.

Then this prayer,

O Lord and heavenly Father, we, thy humble servants, entirely desire thy fatherly goodness, mercifully to accept this our sacrifice of praise and thanksgiving; most humbly beseeching thee to grant, that by the merits and death of thy Son Jesus Christ, and through faith in his blood, we and all thy whole church may obtain remission of our sins, and all other benefits of his passion. And here we offer, and present unto thee, O Lord, ourselves, our souls and bodies, to be a reasonable, holy, and lively sacrifice unto thee; humbly beseeching thee, that all we, who are partakers of this holy communion, may be filled with thy grace and heavenly benediction.

Then was said,

Glory be to God on high, and on earth peace; good will towards men. We praise thee; we bless thee; we worship thee; we glorify thee; we give thanks to thee for thy great glory, O Lord God, heavenly King, God the Father Almighty.

O Lord, the only begotten Son, Jesu Christ.

O Lord God, Lamb of God, Son of the Father, that takest away the sins of the world, have mercy upon us. Thou that takest away the sins of the world, receive our prayer. Thou that sittest at the right hand of God the Father, have mercy upon us.

For thou only art holy, thou only art the Lord, thou only, O Christ, with the Holy Ghost, art most high in the glory of God the Father. Amen.

The King returned to his throne upon the theatre, and afterwards the archbishop read the final prayers.

The Final Prayers.

Assist us mercifully, O Lord, in these our supplications and prayers, and dispose the way of thy servants towards the attainment of everlasting salvation, that, among all the changes and chances of this mortal life, they may ever be defended by thy most gracious and ready help, through Jesus Christ our Lord. Amen.

O Lord our God, who upholdest and governest all things in heaven and earth, receive our humble prayers with our thanksgivings, for our Sovereign Lord George, set over us by thy good providence to be our King: and so, together with him, bless all the Royal Family, that they, ever trusting in thy goodness, protected by thy power, and crowned with thy favour, may continue before thee in health and peace, in joy and honour, a long and happy life upon earth, and after death may obtain everlasting life and glory in the kingdom of heaven, through the merits and mediation of Jesus Christ our Saviour; who with thee, O Father, and the Holy Spirit, liveth and reigneth, ever one God, world without end. Amen.

Almighty God, who hast promised to hear the petition of them that ask in thy Son's name; we beseech thee mercifully to incline thine ears to us that have made now our prayers and supplications unto thee, and grant that those things which we have faithfully asked according to thy will, may effectually be obtained to the relief of our necessity, and to the setting forth of thy glory, through Jesus Christ our Lord. Amen.

The peace of God which passeth all understanding, keep your hearts and minds in the knowledge and love of God, and of his Son Jesus Christ our Lord. And the blessing of God Almighty, the Father, the Son, and the Holy Ghost, be amongst you, and remain with you always. Amen.

The Recess.

The whole coronation office being thus performed, the King, attended and accompanied as before, the four swords being carried before him, descended from his throne crowned, and carrying the sceptre and rod in his hands, went up the area eastward of the theatre, and passed on through the door, on the south side of the altar, into king Edward's chapel; and as they passed by the altar, the rest of the regalia, lying upon it, were delivered by the dean of Westminster to the lords that carried them in the procession, and so they proceeded in state into the chapel; the organ all the while playing.

The King then came into the chapel, and standing before the altar, took off his crown, and delivered it, together with his sceptre, to the archbishop, who laid them upon the altar there; and the rest of the regalia were given into the hands of the dean of Westminster, and by him laid there also.

Then the King withdrew himself into his traverse prepared for him upon the western wall of that chapel.

Within his traverse the King was disrobed by the lord great chamberlain of his royal robe of state (which was forthwith delivered to the dean of Westminster to be laid also upon the altar) and again arrayed with his robe of purple velvet, which was before laid ready in the traverse for that purpose.

When the King, thus habited, came forth of his traverse, he stood before the altar, and the archbishop being still vested in his cope, set the crown of state, provided for the King to wear during the rest of the ceremony, upon his head. Then he gave the sceptre with the cross into the King's right hand, and the orb with the cross into his left: which being done, both the archbishop and dean divested themselves of their copes, and left them there, and proceeded in their usual habits.

Then the King carried his sceptre with the cross in his left hand; the four swords being borne before the King, and the heralds having again put the rest of the procession in order, he went on from king Edward's chapel to the theatre, and thence through the midst of the choir and body of the church, out at the west door, and so returned to Westminster Hall.

Return of the Procession to the Hall.

At about twenty minutes to four the gates of the Hall were thrown open to admit the procession on its return.

The cheering in the Hall on the King's approach was neither so spontaneous nor enthusiastic as it was along the line of march: as far as we could see it originated generally with some of the choristers employed to sing the various portions of the ceremonial.

Viewed from the upper end of the Hall through the arched way, the appearance of the white plumes of the knights of the Bath was most magnificent. On their entrance to the Hall, the knights took off their hats, but the peers continued to wear their coronets. The procession then entered in the following order;—

The King's Herbwoman, with her six Maids.

Messenger of the College of Arms.

High Constable of Westminster.

| Fife and Drums, as before Drum Major Eight Trumpets Kettle Drums Serjeant Trumpeter | } | Who, on arrival in the Hall, immediately went into the Gallery over the Triumphal Arch. |

Serjeant Porter.

Knight Marshal and his Officers.

Six Clerks in Chancery.

King's Chaplains.

Sheriffs of London.

Aldermen and Recorder of London.

Masters in Chancery.

King's Serjeants at Law.

King's Ancient Serjeant.

King's Solicitor-General.   King's Attorney-General.

Gentlemen of the Privy Chamber.

Barons of the Exchequer, and Justices of both Benches.

Lord Chief Baron of the Exchequer

Lord Chief Justice of the Common Pleas.

Vice-Chancellor.   Master of the Rolls.

Lord Chief Justice of the King's Bench.

Pursuivants of Scotland and Ireland.

Officers attendant on the Knights Commanders of the Bath, wearing their Caps.

Knights Commanders of the Bath, wearing their Caps.

Officers of the Order of the Bath, wearing their Caps.

Knights Grand Crosses of the Order of the Bath, wearing their Caps.

A Pursuivant of Arms.

Clerks of the Council in Ordinary.

Privy Counsellors.

Register of the Order of the Garter.

Knight of the Garter, not a Peer, wearing his Cap and Feathers.

His Majesty's Vice-Chamberlain.

Comptroller of the Household.   Treasurer of the Household.

A Pursuivant of Arms.

Heralds or Scotland and Ireland.

The Standard of Hanover, borne by the Earl of Mayo.

Barons, wearing their Coronets.

A Herald.

The Standard of Ireland,	The Standard of Scotland,
borne by	borne by the
Lord Beresford.	Earl of Lauderdale.

Bishops, wearing their Caps.

Two Heralds.

Viscounts, wearing their Coronets.

Two Heralds.

The Standard of England, borne by Lord Hill.

Earls, wearing their Coronets.

Two Heralds.

The Union Standard, borne by Earl Harcourt.

Marquesses, wearing their Coronets.

The Lord Chamberlain of the Household, wearing his Coronet.

The Lord Steward of the Household, wearing his Coronet.

The Royal Standard, borne by the Earl of Harrington.

King of Arms of the Ionian Order of St. Michael & St. George, wearing his Crown.	Gloucester King of Arms, wearing his Crown.	Hanover King of Arms, wearing his Crown.

Dukes, wearing their Coronets.

Ulster King of Arms, wearing his Crown.	Clarenceux King of Arms, wearing his Crown.	Hanover King of Arms, wearing his Crown.

The Lord Privy Seal, wearing his Coronet.	The Lord President of the Council, wearing his Coronet.

Archbishops of Ireland, wearing their Caps.

Archbishop of York, wearing his Cap.

Lord High Chancellor, wearing his Coronet, and bearing his Purse.

Archbishop of Canterbury, wearing his Cap.

Four Serjeants at Arms.

The third Sword, borne by the Earl of Galloway, wearing his Coronet.	Curtana, borne by the Duke of Newcastle, wearing his Coronet.	The Second Sword, borne by the Duke of Northumberland, wearing his Coronet.

Usher of the Green Rod.	Usher of the White Rod.

The Lord Mayor of London.	The Lord Lyon of Scotland	Garter Principal King of Arms, wearing his

wearing his　　　　　　　Crown.
Crown.

The Deputy Lord Great Chamberlain, wearing his Coronet.

His Royal Highness the Prince Leopold, wearing his Cap and Feathers, and his Train borne as before.

His Royal Highness the Duke of Gloucester, wearing his Coronet, and his Train borne as before.

His Royal Highness the Duke of Cambridge, wearing his Coronet, and his Train borne as before.

His Royal Highness the Duke of Sussex, wearing his Coronet, and his Train borne as before.

His Royal Highness the Duke of Clarence, wearing his Coronet, and his Train borne as before.

His Royal Highness the Duke of York, wearing his Coronet, and his Train borne as before.

The High Constable　　The High Constable of Scotland,
of Ireland.　　　　　wearing his Coronet.

Four Serjeants at Arms.

| The Deputy Earl Marshal wearing his coronet. | The sword which had been redeemed, borne naked by the Duke of Dorset, wearing his coronet. The Lord High Steward, wearing his coronet. The Sceptre with the Dove | The Lord High Constable, wearing his coronet. |

borne by
the Duke of Rutland,
wearing his coronet.

The King,

In his Robes of purple velvet, furred with ermine, and the Crown of state on his head, bearing in his right hand St. Edward's Sceptre, with the Cross, and in his left the Orb with the Cross, under his canopy, supported as before, and his train borne as before.

Twenty Gentlemen Pensioners, with the Standard Bearer.

The Bishop of Oxford, wearing his cap.

The Bishop of Lincoln, wearing his cap.

Twenty Gentlemen Pensioners, with the Lieutenant.

Captain of the Yeoman of the Guard, wearing his coronet.

Gold Stick of the Life Guards in waiting, wearing his coronet.

Captain of the Band of Gentlemen Pensioners, wearing his coronet.

Lords of the Bedchamber.

The Keeper of his Majesty's Privy Purse.

Grooms of the Bedchamber.

Equerries and Pages of Honour.

Aides-de-Camp.

Gentlemen Ushers.

Physicians. Surgeons. Apothecaries.

Ensign of the Yeomen of the Guard.   Lieutenant of the Yeomen of the Guard.

His Majesty's Pages.

His Majesty's Footmen.

Exons of the Yeomen of the Guard.   Yeomen of the Guard.   Exons of the Yeomen of the Guard.

Gentleman Harbinger of the Band of Gentlemen Pensioners.

Clerk of the Cheque to the Yeomen of the Guard.   Clerk of the Cheque to the Gentlemen Pensioners.

Yeomen of the Guard, to close the Procession.

As the procession entered the Hall, the fifes, drums, and trumpets went to their gallery, and the several other persons composing it were directed to their respective places by the officers of arms.

On entering the Hall, the barons of the Cinque Ports, bearing the canopy, remained at the bottom of the steps. His Majesty ascended the elevated platform, and retired in his chamber near the state.

The company at the table then sat down; and the barons of the Cinque Ports carried away the canopy as their fee.

It is mentioned above that the several orders of knighthood returned wearing their hats. This was the case until they got to the entrance of Westminster Hall. There all the knights of the Bath took off their hats, as did some of the bishops and several other individuals who took part in the procession. There were only two knights of the Garter who appeared in the full dress of the order. These were his Royal Highness the Prince Leopold and the Marquess of Londonderry. The noble marquess, as attired in his robes, added very considerably to the splendour of the scene by his graceful and elegant appearance. His lordship's hat was encircled with a band of diamonds, which had a most brilliant effect. As his Majesty passed up the Hall he was received with loud and continued acclamations—the gentlemen waving their hats, and the ladies their handkerchiefs: his Majesty seemed to feel sensibly the enthusiasm with which he was greeted, and returned the salutations with repeated bows to the assemblage on both sides. The peers took their seats at the table appointed for them, and began to partake of the banquet. During the interval between this and the return of his Majesty, the greater part of the ladies and gentlemen who had previously occupied the galleries retired for refreshments, or descended into the Hall, which they promenaded for a considerable time. There were also a great number of persons admitted into the Hall, who it was evident had not been in before. This occasioned some slight inconvenience to those whose duty obliged them to be present. We ought here to remark that the procession, on its return to the Hall, was not conducted with any thing like the same regularity which had distinguished its departure. This was probably owing to the great fatigue which all the parties had undergone, and to their consequent anxiety to get to their seats. Some slight derangement was occasioned by the aldermen, who, either from the cause just mentioned, or from a mistake with respect to the regulations of the heralds, had no sooner got within the triumphal arch, than they walked over to one of the tables, leaving several of those behind who ought to have preceded them. This trifling mistake was soon corrected by one of the heralds, who brought the worthy magistrates back to their former station in the procession.

The Banquet.

Precisely at twenty minutes past five the lord great chamberlain issued his orders that the centre of the Hall should be cleared. This direction occasioned much confusion, not only because many strangers had been allowed to enter the lower doors for the purpose of surveying the general arrangements, but because those who had tickets for the galleries had descended in considerable numbers to the floor. Lord Gwydyr was under the necessity of personally exerting his authority, with considerable vehemence, in order to compel the attendants of the earl-marshal to quit situations intended for persons more immediately connected with the ceremony. A long interval now occurred, during which the various officers, and especially the heralds, made the necessary arrangements for the nobility expected to return with his Majesty. During this pause silence was generally preserved, in expectation of the return of his Majesty from his chamber.

The entrance of the King was announced by one of the principal heralds, who was followed into the Hall by the lord great chamberlain and the Dukes of York, Clarence, Cambridge, Sussex, and Gloucester. Prince Leopold had for some time previously been engaged in conversation with some of the foreign ambassadors.

His Majesty returned in the robes with which he had been invested in the Abbey, wearing also the same crown. In his right hand he carried the sceptre, and in his left the orb, which, on taking his seat on the throne, he delivered to two peers stationed at his side for the purpose of receiving them.

The first course was then served up. It consisted of 24 gold covers and dishes, carried by as many gentlemen pensioners: they were preceded by six attendants on the clerk comptroller, by two clerks of the kitchen, who received the dishes from the gentlemen pensioners, by the clerk comptroller, in a velvet gown trimmed with silver lace, by two clerks and the secretary of the Board of Green Cloth, by the comptroller and treasurer of the household, and serjeants at arms with their maces.

Before the dishes were placed upon the table by the two clerks of the kitchen, the great doors at the bottom of the Hall were thrown open to the sound of trumpets and clarionets, and the Duke of Wellington, as lord high constable, the Marquis of Anglesey, as lord high steward, and Lord Howard of Effingham, as deputy earl marshal, entered upon the floor on horseback, remaining for some minutes under the archway. The Duke of Wellington was on the left of the King, the earl marshal on the right, and the Marquess of Anglesey in the centre. The two former were mounted on beautiful white horses gorgeously trapped, and the latter on his favourite dun-coloured Arabian.

The Challenge.

Before the second course, the great gate was thrown open at the sound of trumpets without. The deputy appointed to officiate as King's Champion for the lord of the manor of Scrivelsby, in Lincolnshire, entered the Hall on horseback, in a complete suit of bright armour, between the lord high constable and deputy earl marshal, also on horseback, preceded by —

Two Trumpeters, with the Champion's Arms on their Banners.

The Serjeant Trumpeter, with his Mace on his Shoulder.

Two Serjeants at Arms, with their Maces on their Shoulders.

The Champion's two Esquires, in half Armour, one on the right hand bearing the Champion's Lance, the other on the left hand with the Champion's Target, and the Arms of Dymoke depicted thereon.

A Herald, With a Paper in his hand containing the Challenge.

Then followed: —

The Deputy Earl Marshal, on Horseback, in his Robes and Coronet, with the Earl Marshal's Staff in his Hand, attended by a Page.	The CHAMPION, on Horseback, in a complete suit of bright Armour, with a Gauntlet in his Hand, his Helmet on his Head, adorned with a plume of Feathers.	The Lord High Constable, in his Robes and Coronet, and Collar of his Order, on Horseback, with the Constable's Staff, attended by two Pages.

Four Pages, richly apparelled, attendants on the Champion.

His helmet was of polished steel, surmounted by a full rich bending plume of white ostrich feathers, next of light blue, next red, and lastly of an erect black feather. He seemed rather pale in the face, which was of a resolute cast, and ornamented with handsome mustachios. He sat his horse with ease, and the appearance of great firmness, which was no doubt in part attributable to the enormous weight under which the noble animal that bore him seemed to bend. His armour was extremely massive, and deeply lined and engraven: no part of his body was uncovered; and even the broad circular shoulder blades of the armour were so folded over the cuirass, that in action the body could not but be completely defended at all points. The horse was very richly caparisoned, and wore in his headstall a plume of varied feathers. Nothing could exceed the impression produced by the approach of the champion and his loyal array. Every fair bosom felt an indescribable sensation of mingled surprise, pleasure, and apprehension. It seemed as if they were impressed with a conviction that the defiance might not prove an empty ceremony; that a trial as severe as that of Ivanhoe, in the presence of his future sovereign at Ashby, might await the challenger; and that the nobly-equipped champion before them might, nevertheless, be as little elated by his success, or as faint and feeble when he fell at the feet of sympathising beauty to claim the hard-earned meed of glory. For a moment the fast fading spirit of chivalry re-asserted itself within those walls, over minds which the place and occasion had rendered vividly susceptible of impressions connected with the records of our earlier history.

At the entrance into the Hall the trumpets sounded thrice, and the passage to the king's table being cleared by the knight marshal, the herald, with a loud voice, proclaimed the champion's challenge in the words following:—

If any person, of what degree soever, high or low, shall deny or gainsay our Sovereign Lord George the Fourth of the United Kingdom of Great Britain and Ireland, Defender of the Faith, Son and next Heir to our Sovereign Lord King George the Third, the last King, deceased, to be right Heir to the Imperial Crown of this United Kingdom, or that he ought not to enjoy the same, here is his Champion, who saith that he lieth, and is a false traitor; being ready in person to combat with him, and in this quarrel will adventure his life against him on what day soever he shall be appointed.

The champion then threw down his iron glove or gauntlet; which, having lain for a short time upon the ground, the herald took up, and delivered again to the champion.

They then advanced to the middle of the Hall, where the ceremony was again performed in the same manner.

Lastly, they advanced to the steps of the throne, where the herald (and those who preceded him) ascending to the middle of the steps, proclaimed the challenge in the like manner; when the champion, having thrown down the gauntlet, and received it again from the herald, made a low obeisance to the King, The peers had repeated, as if with one voice, "God bless the King! God save the King!" which was accompanied by acclamations so loud through all parts of the Hall, that it startled the horses of the champion and his noble companions. Then the cupbearer, having received from the officer of the Jewel-house a gold cup and cover filled with wine, presented the same to the King, and his Majesty drank to the champion, and sent to him by the cupbearer the said cup, which the champion (having put on his gauntlet) received, and having made a low obeisance to the King, drank off the wine;

and in a loud articulate voice, exclaimed, turning himself round, "Long life to his Majesty King George the Fourth!" This was followed by a peal of applause resembling thunder; after which, making another low obeisance to his Majesty, and being accompanied as before, he departed out of the Hall, taking with him the said cup and cover as his fee, retiring with his face to his Majesty, and backing his horse out of the Hall.

Proclamaton of the Styles.

Immediately afterwards, Garter, attended by Clarenceux, Norroy, Lyon, Ulster, and the rest of the kings and officers of arms, proclaimed his Majesty's styles in Latin, French, and English, three several times, first upon the uppermost step of the elevated platform, next in the middle of the Hall; and, lastly, at the bottom of the Hall, the officers of arms before each proclamation crying, "Largesse." After each proclamation, the company shouted "God save the King!" and the ladies waved their handkerchiefs and fans.

Second Course.

The second course was then served up with the same ceremony as the first.

Services in Pursuance of Claims.

Then the lord of the manor of Nether Bilsington presented his Majesty with three maple cups.

The office of chief butler of England was executed by the Duke of Norfolk, as Earl of Arundel and lord of the manor of Keninghall, who received a gold basin and ewer as his fee.

Dinner being concluded, the lord mayor and twelve principal citizens of London, as assistants to the chief butler of England, accompanied by the King's cupbearer and assistant, presented to his Majesty wine in a gold cup; and the King having drunk thereof, returned the gold cup to the lord mayor as his fee.

The mayor of Oxford, with the eight other burgesses of that city, as assistants to the lord mayor and citizens of London, as assistant to the chief butler of England in the office of butler, was conducted to his Majesty, preceded by the King's cupbearer, and having presented to the King a bowl of wine, received the three maple cups for his fee.

The lord of the manor of Lyston, pursuant to his claim, then brought up a charger of wafers to his Majesty's table.

The Duke of Athol, as lord of the Isle of Man, presented his Majesty with two falcons. Considerable curiosity was excited by the presentment of these beautiful birds, which sat perfectly tame on the arm of his grace, completely hooded, and furnished with bells.

The Duke of Montrose, as master of the horse to the King, performed the office of serjeant of the silver scullery.

The lord of the barony of Bedford performed the office of almoner; and the office of chief larderer was performed by the deputy of the Earl of Abergavenny.

After the dessert was served up, the King's health was announced by the peers, and drank by them and the whole of the persons in the Hall standing, with three times three. The lord chancellor, overpowered by his feelings on this propitious occasion, rose, and said it was usual to drink the health of a subject with three times three, and he thought that his subjects ought to drink the Sovereign's health with nine times nine. The choir and additional singers had now been brought forward in front of the knights commanders, and the national anthem of "God save the King" was sung with incomparable effect.

The Duke of Norfolk then said, "The King thanks his peers for drinking his health: he does them the honour to drink their health and that of his good people." His Majesty rose, and bowing three times to various parts of the immense concourse —

— — "The abstract of his kingdom,"

he drank the health of all present. It was succeeded by long and continued shouts from all present, during which the King resumed his seat on his throne.

The King quitted the Hall at a quarter before eight o'clock; afterwards the company was indiscriminately admitted to partake of such refreshments as remained on the tables of the peers.

During Tuesday and Wednesday night, in order that no unnecessary interruption might be experienced in the public thoroughfares during the daytime, the workmen under the direction of the Board of Works were busily engaged in raising barriers at different points that commanded the streets and passes leading to Westminster Hall and Abbey. From Charing Cross, a stout barrier was placed (about fifteen feet from the pavement) to Parliament Street, so that the fullest possible room, about twenty feet in width, should be secured for persons having tickets of admission to the Hall, the Abbey, or the Coronation Galleries. And a still stronger barrier was raised along the centre of Parliament Street, one side only being appropriated to carriages going towards the scene of universal attraction. Across Bridge Street, as well as in King Street, and the neighbouring thoroughfares, all the carriage entrances were wholly blockaded; thus securing the most commodious means to persons proceeding on foot to the different places for which they possessed admission tickets. At all these points were stationed constables, supported by parties of military; and at the several passes were placed experienced individuals who had been instructed in their various duties during several days by Mr. Jackson and others, in the long chambers of the House of Lords, &c. They examined the tickets and the pretensions of the several persons applying to pass on to the Abbey, Hall, houses, or galleries. — Still more effectually to qualify them for this duty, they were previously made acquainted with the mode in which the various tickets of the lord great chamberlain (Lord Gwydyr) for the Hall, and the earl marshal of England (Lord Howard, of Effingham, acting deputy), were prepared, signed, and superscribed. — They were also provided with good general means of judging of the authenticity of cards for the different galleries; and even to be guarded against imposture, there was further authority to keep all the several parties in motion, till they arrived at their respective destinations. Thus, every arrangement was made to accomplish the great advantage of clear roads and facilities of approach; and the regulations adopted at those points, passes, and barriers already noticed, were provided at the other stations.

All the arrangements were finally made on Wednesday night. The high bailiff of Westminster (A. Morris, Esq.), the high constable (Mr. Lee), and the several magistrates of the different Police Offices, Sir Robert Baker, Mr. Birnie, Mr. Mainwaring, Mr. Raynsford, Mr. Markland, &c. under the advice, and with the approbation of Lord Sidmouth, agreed upon and adopted at the office of the home secretary of state, a plan of general and particular operations. Each magistrate had his different station allotted to him, with a specified number of the police officers to attend his commands, and enforce his instructions.

Besides the precautions taken in the several streets, and at the various thoroughfares, as already described, arrangements of a similar character were adopted at the several approaches from the river Thames. In the course of the night, the stairs, landing-places, roads from wharfs, &c., along the Westminster side of the banks of the Thames, were closed, with parties to command them, from the Hungerford to the Horseferry stairs. Some exceptions were made regarding the stairs at Whitehall, by Lord Liverpool's house, and a temporary landing-place formed in the course of Wednesday, at the lower end of the speaker's garden, for the accommodation of the treasury and ordnance barges, conveying certain great officers of state, some parties of peeresses, &c., as well as the barges of the lord mayor, aldermen, sheriffs, and twelve citizens of London, accompanied as they were (by the special favour of the corporation of London) by the mayor of Oxford, its recorder, two aldermen, two assistants, &c. And at this entrance proper precautions were taken by stationing a civil force in the speaker's gardens; while in the river, such regulations were strengthened by the parties on board the Thames police-boat, and a gun-brig moored off this point in the course of Wednesday.

The Platform.

The temporary boarding placed up on each side of the platform, some weeks ago, to prevent damage, by indiscriminate visitors travelling over it day and night, was completely removed in the early part of the morning. On the removal of such boarding, the platform presented a lively and finished appearance. The railing on each side of it was covered with purple cloth, and the flooring covered to the extent of sixteen feet, leaving about a yard on each side uncovered, with the same sort of blue cloth.

The awnings were drawn, but at short distances red lines were placed, by the pulling of which command was had of them, to close or spread them as circumstances might require. To each line and pulley was allotted one man, with a particular dress, so that the most rapid change of the awnings could be effected, should the weather require any change in their position, while the addition of a staff enabled such man likewise to act as a constable. There were also placed, on each side of the platform, along the whole range of it, men provided with pincers, hammers, &c., to repair any damage that might happen to the platform, or whatever was calculated to impede the progress of the procession, and its attendant ceremonies. These men were also supplied with a like livery, with staves of office; and they were sworn as constables.

The flooring of the platform was raised several feet (in some instances as much as four and five feet) from the roads; and the side platform was nearly two feet below the surface of the main platform. Thus the view of what excited the greatest curiosity, was not intercepted by the means so judiciously arranged to preserve that regularity and order which so essentially contribute to the effect of all ceremonies.

Coronaton Galleries.

The immense range of galleries in the fronts of houses in New Palace Yard, along the Exchequer Offices and Chambers, over the champion's stables, in Parliament Street and Square, in

George Street, in St. Margaret's Churchyard, in the large spaces, on gardens and squares, between the Parliament House and Sessions House, it would be impossible to particularise. The magnitude of these accommodations, their uniformity and convenience, excited the wonder of the inhabitants of this great metropolis, and of thousands from all parts of the country, who repaired to town solely with the view of witnessing the preparations. All these galleries underwent the strictest investigation by surveyors appointed for the purpose; so that all possible precautions to prevent accidents were adopted.

Westminster Hall.

The preparations within the Hall have on former occasions been fully described, and a tolerably correct notion may be formed by many of the main outlines of the arrangements there, to give effect to the ceremonies preceding, and the banquet following, his Majesty's coronation. The *coup d'œil* was of the most pleasing and imposing character; the galleries along each side of the Hall, the tower and turrets over the grand entrance, and the royal platform and table, were finished in the highest order. The new windows in the roof, and the recently-completed lantern upwards of forty feet high on the centre of the ridge of the roof, with glazed windows all round, greatly improved the effect.

From each side of the angles formed by the ends of the hammer-beams in the roof was suspended by a gilt chain a large splendid cut-glass lustre, with broad ornamented gilt irons and frames, containing three circles of wax candles, being between forty and fifty in each lustre.

The first and second galleries had the mattings and scarlet coverings completed only on Wednesday. The royal box on the right, and the foreigners' box on the left side of the royal table were entirely lined with scarlet cloth, festooned in front, and ornamented with gold fringe.

The throne, seat, and the royal table, attracted general admiration. With the exception of the large fluted columns, the royal seat and canopy were in the style of the throne in the House of Lords. The back of crimson velvet, with the royal arms embroidered on it, and the limits decorated with gold and ornaments. The canopy was square, with a raised and variegated gold cornice round. The centre displayed a splendid crown, underneath which were G. R. IV. Underneath the cornice was a crimson velvet vallance, separated into divisions, the lower portion of each division being rounded with gold, while its centre was decorated with gold, embroidered, and raised ornaments illustrative of the military orders, and of the emblems of the United Kingdom, the Rose, the Thistle, the Harp, &c. The chair was equally splendid; the arms and legs consisting of rich carved work gilt, with crimson velvet back, also ornamented. The only objection in point of taste that can be made to this is, that the glitter did not harmonize with the sober grandeur of the Hall.

About nine o'clock on Wednesday night the King left Carlton Palace for the house of the speaker of the House of Commons in Palace Yard, where his Majesty slept on Wednesday night. His Majesty's coach was escorted by a strong detachment of the Oxford Blues, accoutred as cuirassiers. They made a most beautiful appearance. The carriage drove at a rapid rate across the Parade in St. James's Park, through Storey's Gate and Great George Street. His Majesty was recognised by the crowd on his passage, and saluted with every expression of loyalty and attachment. Prior to the departure of his Majesty from Carlton Palace the crowd between Storey's Gate and Westminster Hall had been cleared by the Scots Greys, so as to make a convenient passage for the carriage, and his Majesty did not set out until after an officer had arrived at the Palace gate to announce that all was ready. His Majesty was guarded through the night by the lord great chamberlain and the usher of the black rod. There were no preparations of importance. His Majesty's sofa bed was brought from Carlton House. On Thursday morning the lord great chamberlain, at seven o'clock, carried to his Majesty his shirt and apparel, and with the lord chamberlain of the household dressed his Majesty. His Majesty then breakfasted, and afterwards proceeded to his chamber, near the south entrance into Westminster Hall.

We entered the Hall at twenty minutes past five o'clock, and a crowd of ladies admitted by peers' orders, and peeresses, were then struggling for admittance.

The first thing we observed on having entered the Hall, was the canopy which was to be borne over the King by the barons of the Cinque Ports. The canopy was yellow;—of silk and gold embroidery, with short curtains of muslin spangled with gold. Eight bearers having fixed the poles by which the canopy was supported, which were of steel (apparently), with silver knobs, bore it up and down the Hall, to practise the mode of carrying it in procession. It was then deposited at the upper end of the side table of the Hall, to the left of the throne. The canopy was not very elegant in form, and did not seem very well calculated to add to the effect of the procession. But even at this early hour the appearance of the Hall, studded with groups of gentlemen pensioners, and various other attendants, in their fantastic and antique costumes, with the officers of the guards, and others, in military uniform, and, above all, the elegantly dressed women who began to fill the galleries, was altogether superb. At this time there were several hundreds of spectators in the Hall.

The sides of the upper end of the Hall, including the boxes for the foreign ministers and royal family, were hung with scarlet cloth, edged with gold.

The throne was splendid with gold and crimson; the canopy over the throne was of crimson and gold, with the royal arms in embroidery. The large square table before the throne, intended for the display of the regalia, was of purple, having a rim of gold, and an interior square moulding of the same description, about two feet from the edge. The platform on which the throne was placed, and the three steps immediately descending from it, were covered with brown carpeting; the two other descending flights of steps, and the double chairs, placed by the side of the tables for the peers (with the names of their future occupiers), and the coverings of the railings in front of the seats, were of morone cloth. From the bottom of the steps, descending from the throne to the north gate, the middle of the floor of the Hall was covered with blue cloth, in the same manner as the platform without. The rest of the floor and the seats were matted. The side tables were covered with green cloth; and as on each side, the galleries reached nearly to the top of the windows in the wall, only the upper arches of those windows, and the noble roof of the old fabric appeared, except at each end, the upper one especially, where the grave visages of the Saxon kings, newly decorated, made their appearance. The light, which was only admitted from the roof windows, and from those in each end, though sober, was, on the whole, good. At the lower end the attendants of the earl marshal attracted some notice by their dark dresses, with white sashes, stockings, shoes with large rosettes, and Queen Elizabeth ruffs, with gilt staves tipped with black. At a quarter after seven o'clock an attendant, habited in the dress of *Henri Quatre* laid on the table, near the canopy, eight maces, to be borne in the course of the procession.

Her Royal Highness the Duchess of Gloucester was the first of the royal family who arrived in the Hall; taking her seat in the royal box at a quarter before six. Her Royal Highness was splendidly attired in a rich dress of silver lama over French lilac; head-dress, a white satin hat, with an elegant plume of white feathers, turned up with a diamond button and loop in front; and appeared to be in excellent health and spirits.

Soon afterwards the Duchess of Clarence entered the Hall, and took her seat next to her royal sister-in-law, the Duchess of Gloucester. About half past seven their Royal Highnesses the Duchess of Kent, the Princess Sophia of Gloucester, and the Princess Feodore (daughter of the Duchess of Kent) took their seats in the royal box. Their Royal Highnesses were attired in splendid dresses of white satin, richly embroidered in silver, with rich bandeau head-dresses, and large plumes of white feathers.

The herb-women entered the Hall from the south end before eight o'clock. Miss Fellowes, the principal herb-woman, was led in by Mr. Fellowes; and the six young ladies, her assistants, followed two and two. They were afterwards seated at the north entrance of the Hall. They were elegantly dressed in white, tastefully decorated with flowers. Miss Fellowes wore, in addition to the same dress, a scarlet mantle. At eight o'clock three large baskets were brought into the Hall, filled with flowers, for them to bear. Of a very different description from these were some persons who were observed in various parts of the Hall. These were well-known prize-fighters, who were stationed from an idea of the necessity of keeping peace among the honourable and noble throng. We observed Cribb, Randall, Richmond, and we understood many others were present.

The canopy was removed at eight o'clock from the side table where it had been placed, and was brought into the middle of the Hall. The barons of the Cinque Ports were then marshalled, two to each pole; they then bore the canopy down the Hall by way of practice, according to a word of command. — Some laughter was at first excited by the irregular manner in which the bearers moved. Their dresses were, however, extremely splendid — large cloaks of garter-blue satin, with slashed arms of scarlet, and stockings of dead red.

Many peers had been occasionally in the Hall at a very early hour in the morning, and before eight o'clock they had all arrived at the buildings near the House of Lords, and took their coronets and robes. The archbishops and bishops assembled about the same time, and vested themselves in their rochets, in the House of Lords and chambers adjacent. The judges, and others of the long robe, together with the gentlemen of the privy chamber, esquires of the body, serjeants at law, masters in chancery, aldermen of London, chaplains having dignities, and six clerks in chancery, being all in their proper habits, assembled at the places, of which notice has been given, where the officers of arms arranged them according to their respective classes, four in a rank, placing the youngest on the left, and then conducted them into the Hall.

The King's serjeants were in red gowns. The masters in chancery (nine of whom attended) were in the dress in which they attend the house of lords.

The barons of the Cinque Ports took a second turn in the Hall, which, as it began with more formality, was attended with more laughter than the first. About this time also the four swords were brought in, and deposited on the end of the left hand table, with the spurs, and a cushion for the crown. The knights of the Bath now began to assemble, and with the others who were to take part in the procession, were ranged at the end of the Hall. The dresses of the knights of the Bath were extremely splendid, but somewhat gaudy. The knights had all close dresses of white satin, puckered in a variety of ways. The grand crosses wore flowing robes of pinkish red satin, lined with white; the commanders small mantles. The judges and privy counsellors, not being peers, next entered; the latter in splendid dresses of blue velvet and gold.

Among them were the Earl of Yarmouth, Lord Binning, Mr. Canning, Mr. Bathurst, Mr. Huskisson, Sir G. Hill, Mr. Robinson, Mr. Beckett, Lord G. Beresford, and Mr. Wallace.

The barons then entered, Lords Stowell and Maryborough (late Sir W. Scott and W. W. Pole), being among the first. There were but forty-nine (if we rightly counted them) present. Next came the bishops—fifteen attended; the viscounts, nineteen in number. The earls were more numerous—we should think seventy or eighty; but the Hall now became so crowded that there was a difficulty in counting them accurately. The marquesses and dukes, and lastly the great officers of state, archbishops, and members of the royal family, entered. Prince Leopold of Saxe-Cobourg was in the full robes of the order of the Garter. The princes of the blood and some of the dukes placed themselves on the right of the platform about the throne. The marquesses and some of the earls on the left side, formed a line with those who had descended to the floor of the Hall. The show of ermine and velvet on the descent of the platform was of the most magnificent description.

A herald then went through the line of peers, marshalling each according to the order of their creation—the junior first. They were a second time called over, and ranged in a double file on each side of the middle space of the Hall by Mr. Mash.

Before the King entered, the peers were all ranged on each side of the Hall, none being left on the platform but the great officers of state and the royal family.

Precisely at ten o'clock the King entered the Hall from the door behind the throne, habited in robes of enormous size and richness, wearing a black hat with a monstrous plume of ostrich feathers, out of the midst of which rose a black heron's plume. His Majesty seemed very much oppressed with the weight of his robes. The train was of enormous length and breadth. It was of crimson velvet adorned with large golden stars, and a broad golden border. His Majesty frequently wiped his face while he remained seated. He went through the ceremonies, which we have described, with much spirit and apparent good humour. In descending the steps of the platform his Majesty seemed very feeble, and requested the aid and support of an officer who was near him. Instead of standing under the canopy, his Majesty, perhaps afraid of the awkwardness of the barons, preceded it. The canopy was therefore always borne after him. When his Majesty had got a little way down the Hall, he turned to his train-bearers, and requested them to bear his train farther from him, apparently with a view to relieve himself from the weight. As he went down the Hall he conversed with much apparent cheerfulness with the bishop of Lincoln, who was on his right hand.

It will behove the historian to record the unsuccessful attempts of her Majesty to obtain the usual honour of Queen-Consort on the preceding occasion, *i.e.* that of a joint coronation with her husband; and too much public attention was excited to the subject at the period of the coronation to render our sketch of that august ceremony complete without adverting to it.

Her Majesty first presented a memorial, desiring to know in what way she was to attend the coronation; to which it was replied, that it rested with the King to nominate who should be present, and his Majesty was advised that he could not allow her to be present.

The Queen rejoined, that she should be present if not absolutely prohibited; and it was farther replied, that his Majesty's ministers advised that she could not be received.

She now prayed the King in council (July 1) to be heard by her legal advisers against this decision—a request which was granted "as matter of *favour*," according to the language of the minister, "but not of right;" and, on Thursday, July 5, at ten o'clock in the morning, the Privy Council met at Whitehall to hear her Majesty's claim argued. For many years so large a Privy Council had not met, there being forty-nine members present, besides a considerable number of members of parliament not of the council.

Mr. Brougham, after stating the refusal of the dean and chapter of Westminster to grant him the use of the *"Liber Regalis"* (a formula of the coronation ceremony in their custody), and having induced the president to send for that volume, commenced by observing:

That "the King had the right of being crowned," was a proposition which he thought he should have no difficulty of supporting; and that the Queen enjoyed the same right, he thought he could establish upon exactly the same legal ground. The ground upon which he mainly relied was a uniform, uninterrupted practice, in the sense in which he thought he should be permitted to use and avail himself of these terms in a court of justice, and in which he should be justified in establishing out of them the legal existence of any private right. That some interruptions had arisen in this uniform practice he was prepared to admit and explain, for they were such as did not affect the uninterrupted right; but, in the mode in which he had to account for them, rather sanctioned and confirmed it. There would be two propositions which he entreated their lordships to bear in mind while he went through his narrative of historical facts. The first was the uniform exercise of the right; namely, that no king had ever been crowned, being married at the time of his coronation, without the queen-consort herself partaking with the king in the solemnity of the coronation; and, secondly, that there never was a queen-consort in England who had not partaken of the ceremony of the coronation: but in making these two propositions, he begged of course to be understood, as using them subject to the usual qualifications of general propositions; which were—being bound to show that where any interruptions had existed, they did not compromise the general right. With interruptions, as to the first proposition, he had but one to contend, which was capable of easy solution. As to the second, he could easily and satisfactorily explain whatever exceptions had arisen, for they were few, and tended to confirm the right of the Queen-Consort. The learned gentleman then proceeded to call the attention of the lords of the council to various records which he quoted from English history, in order to establish his proposition,—the right of British queens to be crowned, from the year 784, through the Saxon and Norman lines, down to the house of Tudor. In Henry the Second's reign a remarkable circumstance occurred: the solemnity of crowning his eldest son took place in his father's life-time; the prince was married to a daughter of Louis of France, and she was not crowned although her husband was. The novelty of that omission of what was considered a uniform ceremony, led to a complaint and remonstrance to the king of England, and the result was, that he had recourse for redress to the usual process of kings—to arms, and a declaration of war; and in front of his reasons for taking that step, the French king placed the omission to crown his daughter with her husband. Henry was at length obliged to submit, for he went over to France and entered into some compromise with Louis to avert hostilities, and the daughter of the French king was solemnly crowned at Winchester by bishops and other venerable and distinguished authorities, who were sent over from France to perform the ceremony of her coronation with suitable splendour.

On arriving at the era of Henry the Sixth, the learned counsel said he should refer to the law of Scotland about the period of history at which he was passing. The Scottish documents contained enough to establish the fact, that no king of Scotland who was married at the time of his coronation was ever crowned without his consort; nor, where the marriage took place afterwards, was there an instance in which a Scottish queen was not crowned as soon as possible after she became queen. The learned counsel then referred to the act 1428 in the Scottish statutes, cap. 109, passed in the eighth parliament of James the First, and read the "aith to be made to the queen, be the clergie and the baronnes."

The case of Henry the Seventh's queen was next quoted. She had been crowned two years after the king's coronation. This coronation was announced by proclamation similar to that which had announced his own two years and a month before; and the order of it, as would be seen in the Close Roll, and in Rymer, was similar to that observed at all other coronations of queens-consort. The varying conduct of Henry the Eighth with regard to his queens was then accounted for. Charles the First was crowned without his queen, because of the antipathy of the people against the papists, of whom she was one; yet only nine days before he was himself crowned, a proclamation was issued for the crowning of his queen, but observing the popular feeling to be against such a measure, that ceremony was postponed. The queen was said to have objected to take any part in the coronation unless she could be assisted in it by a popish priest, which the constitution of the country rendered absolutely impossible. The same reasons operated against the crowning of Charles the Second's queen, who was also a papist. James the Second and his queen were crowned together, although they were both Roman Catholics. If he and his consort could reconcile it to themselves to go into a Protestant cathedral, and to partake in the ceremonies of a Protestant ritual, there was an end of the difficulty which he had described as originating from the words of one of the oaths having one sense to one of the parties who took them, and another to the other. Since the revolution every thing regarding this subject was well known, and every king and queen had been regularly crowned. With regard to the queen of George the First, he must beg leave to observe, that as she had never been in this country, he had nothing to do with her. Besides, she was said to have been divorced from her husband by the sentence of a foreign ecclesiastical court before he ascended the throne of this country; so that it was legally impossible that she could be crowned if she had been divorced from her husband, and physically impossible if she had never set foot in the country. Her case, therefore, formed no exception to her present Majesty's right. Whilst he was upon this subject he might be permitted to remark, as not extraneous to it, that he had not expected and did not expect to hear in that court, as a bar to her Majesty's claim, that some proceedings had been instituted against her. He made that assertion not on his own authority, but on the authority of a noble and learned judge, who, in giving sentence on the King and Wolfe, in the court of the highest resort in the country, had said, in consequence of some observations having been made as to the defendant having been guilty of some great offence, "If a man be guilty of ever so great an offence, and the proceedings against him fail in substantiating that offence, he is to be considered in law as innocent as if no such offence had ever been charged against him."

Friday, July 6.—Mr. Brougham rose at a few minutes after ten to resume his speech. He had yesterday gone through a long and unbroken series of precedents, showing that no king of England had ever been crowned, he being married at the time of his coronation, without his consort participating in that ceremony. Having gone so far, he contended that he had a right to assume his larger proposition, that queens-consort had, at all times throughout the ages of English history, themselves enjoyed the ceremony of the coronation. If in one or two instances this was not done at the time when the king's own coronation took place, and supposing that there was an instance or two where the queen-consort became such after the coronation of the king, still he would affirm, that according to all the rules of argument, of law, and of common sense, those few instances, (admitting there were some, though in point of strict fact he believed there were none,) did not in any manner or degree affect his general argument, which he held upon the authorities he had cited to be altogether incontrovertible. He was not before their lordships to show where the right which he asserted in behalf of the queen-consort had been claimed and refused. In every instance, in which it was actually possible for a coronation of a queen to take place, he had shown that it had been solemnized. There was not a single case which, *quoad* that case, cast a doubt upon the uniform force of his proposition, except that of Henrietta Maria, wife of Charles the First; and he reminded their lordships, it was merely a doubt so far as that particular case went. He had a right then to assume the larger proposition, that all queens-consort of England had, in point of fact, been crowned. Nothing was clearer in the rules of equity and law, than that non-uses did not forfeit, unless where they clearly, from the length of the lapse, involved a waiver of the claim. Where a right had been disputed, and the opposition assented to by the party tacitly, or confirmed by a competent authority, then, of course, there was an end to the legal exercise of such a right. But here the very reverse was the fact. Suppose he were called upon to prove a right of way or a right of common, (the two instances in which the courts of law were most commonly called upon to consider the length of usage,) the principle of law would go with the uniformity, and the absence of exercising the right in one or two particular instances would prove nothing. There were three modes of calling into question the fact of usage; *first*, as to its uniform enjoyment; *next*, where the right claimed by the party had been contested, but nevertheless enjoyed by the person exercising it; and the *third* case was, where the right asserted had been confiscated, and an adjudication passed upon it: that was of course held to be conclusive against the party, where the right claimed was refused, opposed, and not acquiesced in; then he admitted that no long admission of the right could be pleaded without the fatal interruption of the bar. He entreated their lordships to try the usage of the coronation of the queen-consort by these three principles of investigating such rights founded upon immemorial custom. Of the first, namely, uniform enjoyment, they had abundant proof. As to the second, namely, the occurrence of interruption in the exercise of the right, non-acquiescence in that interruption, a successful and most complete resistance to the attempt to withhold the exercise of the right, they had that, fully sustaining his proposition, in the case of the wife of Prince Henry; where Henry thought proper in his lifetime to crown his eldest son without also crowning that eldest son's consort. He had therefore with him the uniform enjoyment of the right her Majesty claimed; then the successful resistance of an attempt, as in Henry's case, to delay the exercise of the right; and lastly, the total absence of any adjudication or confiscation, or any thing like either in any single instance against him. There was, in fact, no other possible way of showing the existence of the right, but in the manner in which he was assuming, proving, and, as he thought, establishing it. How else, before the Court of Claims, were rights of service at the ceremony of the coronation established? How else did the barons of the Cinque Ports show their right to carry the canopy over the king, and to have a part of that canopy for their service? Suppose any instance in which the barons should, for want of specific proof, in the lapse of ages, fail to show that they had exercised that privilege—would that countervail the validity of their claim, founded on repeated usage? Certainly not. He would venture to say that there were at least half a dozen instances in which the barons could not show they had exercised their asserted right: and would any of these instances, where that proof failed, shake the firm hold of their long and undeniable usage? Upon a reference to the services which were to be performed at the ceremony of the coronation, it was clear, from the separate rights held upon the performance of particular kinds of attendance upon the queen, that her part of the ceremony was substantive, independent, and principal; that her right was clearly within herself, and not dependent upon the mere will of the King. So essential, indeed, was it that she should be crowned with all the forms of pomp which belonged to such a solemnity, that the same writs of summons were issued, and nearly the same demands of service made upon officers of state as when the king himself was crowned. The usage clearly governed the right, and more especially in this solemnity of coronation, which was altogether the creature of precedent, and existed only by its authority. The queen's coronation was in itself manifestly a substantive, important, and independent ceremony, illustrative of the right of the one party, and not dependent or contingent upon the mere will of the monarch. The origin of the king's ceremonial was lost in remote antiquity; but the numerous tenures and dependencies determinable by the non-performance of services at the solemnity, showed how important it was intended to be in the eyes of the people. The only grounds of right for the king's coronation, the queen equally had for hers; and there were, as he had already stated, separate forms prescribed for those who were officially to attend her ceremony.

The learned counsel then quoted some passages from the *Liber Regalis*, being merely directions for particular parts of the ceremonial to be observed on the queen's coronation. Every solemnity of which the origin was lost in distant antiquity, which was in itself of a most high and public nature, and which occupied a great and important space in the history of the country, he would fearlessly assert, must be deemed and taken as the right of the realm, and not as a mere appanage of the king. He held the coronation of the king himself to be a right of this nature; and that, not merely in the present times on account of the coronation oath, (which had been devised by the legislature on the coronation of William and Mary,) but also in times long before them: indeed, it had always been considered as a high and august ceremony with which the monarch himself could not dispense; it being the right of the sovereign, not in his individual but in his political capacity, for the benefit of the whole nation, in which capacity alone the nation knew him at his coronation. So much with regard to the coronation of the king. The coronation of the queen ought to be considered in a similar light, from its having been celebrated almost without interruption with the same publicity, and from being in its nature such as he had repeatedly described it. The king and the queen being both of them the mere creations of the law, the solemnities of their coronations were mere creations of the law also, and were known to it in no other light than as the rights of the whole realm of England. He, therefore, who was ready to take one step, and to get rid of the queen's coronation, as a mere optional ceremony, ought to be ready to take also another step, and to get rid of the king's coronation, on the ground of its being a vain, idle, empty, and expensive pageant. Her claim to a coronation rested upon immemorial usage, and the numerous rights of individuals which were interwoven and connected with it. Indeed, it rested on the same foundation as the king's: it was supported by the same arguments, and the interruptions which it had experienced admitted of the same explanations that he had given to those which had occurred in the case of the king. He had mentioned, in the course of his argument, the rights which belonged to other individuals in consequence of the queen's right to a coronation. If a coronation was not granted to her Majesty, their rights were unavailing to them; and that, in his opinion, formed a very sufficient reason why it should be celebrated. That the coronation was the acknowledgment of the king by the people, he conceived to be a point which it was unnecessary to prove to their lordships: but he might be permitted to remark to them, that the coronation of the queen was even considered as an acknowledgment of her right to enjoy that dignity in an entry in a charter roll of the fifth year of King John, now preserved in the Tower. The entry to which he alluded was the grant of certain lands in dower to his Queen Isabella, and it referred by way of recital to her coronation as queen. This excerpt was of no small importance in the consideration of this question; for it proved to their lordships, that in times when the coronation of the king was positively either his election, or the recognition of his election as monarch, the coronation of the queen was conducted, for the very same reasons, with the same solemnities. This was evident from the description of what was done, and from the manner and the avowed object of doing it. John was crowned to show that he was king—"*coronatus in regem.*" Isabella was crowned to show that she was queen—"*in reginam coronata communi consensu archiepiscoporum,*" &c. &c. The very same persons who elected, or recognised, or only crowned him as their monarch, are, in this passage, recorded to have elected, or recognised, or only crowned her as their queen. Was it intended to be maintained that no right existed, whenever something moving from the crown was necessary to the exercise of it? He would frankly confess that he knew of no right which a subject could enjoy without the interposition of the crown in some manner or other. All writs issued from the crown, and no right could be maintained without them; yet, would any one dispute the right of the subject to obtain them? Supposing a peer were to die, and the crown were to refuse a writ of summons to his eldest son: it was said to be by petition of right alone that he could sue to the crown to be admitted to his father's honours; and yet that petition of right would be considered as a strict undeniable legal right. He could refer also to cases in which the subject could demand, not merely the king's writ, but also the king's proclamation, to which he was entitled, not by a common law right, but by a right given him by an express statute; for instance, in all cases relative to prize-money. Again, supposing that the House of Commons were to die a natural death after sitting for seven years, and the king were to refuse to issue his proclamation to convoke another within three years of that period, as ordered by the first of William and Mary, sec. 2, cap. 2, would it be asserted that the subject would have no right to call for the proclamation of the king to convoke another parliament, because such proclamation could not issue without an act of the crown? He thought that none of their lordships would advocate such an absurdity. But the subject and the country were in full possession of all these rights; and if the Queen's right to a coronation were put upon the same footing, it would be equally clear that she possessed it, and that the necessity of granting it was as obvious as it was imperative. He had heard it said that her Majesty could not claim the honours of a coronation by prescription, because she was not a corporation. This, however, he denied. Her Majesty certainly could prescribe, for what business had they to call her Majesty less a corporation than the King? But still, supposing her not to be a corporation, she had a right to prescribe as a functionary, holding a high dignity and situation. This was evident from Baron Comyn's Digest, who, under the title of *Prescription*, lays it down that such a functionary can claim by prescription. In conclusion, Mr. Brougham said, their lordships would sit in dignified judgment on the opinion given by the great lawyers of the nineteenth century; and, as he firmly believed, finding they had no difficulties to explain, perceiving that they had no obscurities to clear up, they would not be under the necessity of referring to those remote periods of our history, to which he had been obliged to allude, but would look back to the first decision that ever had been given on this question, with that decided confidence which the names of those privy counsellors before whom the case was argued would in after-times command—a judgment, which he ventured confidently to pronounce, would not derogate from the high character they had so long maintained.

Mr. Denman followed on the same side, and after a long speech, called on their lordships, as a court sitting for legal inquiry, to say whether there ever was a case presented to an inquest, which depended on custom and usage, where a more complete and perfect body of custom and usage had been adduced, than was brought forward on the present occasion? If her Majesty's claim were refused, no dignity was safe, no property was secure, not a single institution could be said to rest on a firm foundation. If the coronation of the Queen could not be supported by custom, the rest of that ceremonial could not be supported. Why was this country governed by a king? Why did we submit to a kingly government? Because the earliest ages, because all times, had recognised that form of government, and because we could trace that custom beyond all time of memory. Nothing could be more dangerous than to separate royalty from the circumstances which belonged to it and added to its dignity. The lives and properties of men depended for their security upon the same principle. Why was there a house of peers, in which noble lords formed a part of the legislature? Why were there commoners, who sat as representatives of the people? Precisely because custom had ordered it so. Custom was the author of the law and the law-makers. Custom authorized the king, lords, and commons, to enact laws for the government of this realm. All property, all dignity, all offices existed, because they were sanctioned by prescriptive custom, or because custom gave a prescriptive right to create them.

Saturday.—The Privy Council resumed this morning, soon after ten o'clock. Below the bar was again crowded to excess.

Counsel were then called in.

Mr. Brougham said, he now held in his hand, and was prepared to lay before the council, the documentary evidence to which he and his learned friend had adverted in the course of their addresses in support of her Majesty's memorial.

Lord Harrowby.—Mr. Attorney-General, have you any observations to offer on what counsel have stated to their lordships?

The Attorney-General then rose.—He said, he perhaps should best discharge his duty by stating, at the commencement, that, in his own opinion, the argument and claim were wholly unfounded. That the claim was not founded on any recognised law, appeared from the statements and course of proceeding adopted by her Majesty's counsel. He would add, that the claim now made, so far from ever being supposed to have any foundation, was not even mentioned by any writer on the laws and constitution. It had never been agitated or alluded to in any way, not even by those writers who had touched on the privileges peculiar to a queen-consort. The one single ground urged in support of the claim was usage—that usage was supposed to have prevailed through a long series of years at the coronation of kings who were married. It had been stated with confidence that such usage was evidence in support of the right; but when they were talking of rights founded on usage, it was not sufficient to state that particular facts had taken place. In all such cases, where the facts were relied on, it was essential to state the circumstances that had attended such facts, the peculiarities that had accompanied the alleged privilege, whether it was right of way or otherwise. As to the right of way, for instance; if permission were given to use certain paths or roads, the fact of such permission having preceded the use, at once destroyed the claim of right. If the license and permission were proved, there was an end of the right. By that proof, all the inferences drawn from the use were at an end—they were at once destroyed. The coronation was for the purpose of the monarch's recognition by the people, and on the part of the king to enter into the solemn compact to preserve the laws. The coronation of a queen was a mere ceremony; but that of the king was something more than ceremony. His coronation was accompanied by important political acts—the recognition by the people, and, on the other hand, the solemn compact entered into by the sovereign to preserve and maintain the laws of the realm. Still, however, as far as the king was concerned, it was a ceremony; it was not necessary to the sovereign's possession of the crown—it was what proceeded from his will, and might be dispensed with. But the queen-consort, who filled no political character in the state, had only enjoyed the privilege because she was the king's consort. With respect to a queen-consort, when she was crowned, there was no recognition of her by the people, no compact towards the people. There was no engagement between her and the subjects of the realm. This fact established that, with respect to a queen-consort, a coronation was an honorary ceremony, unaccompanied by any acts. That the coronation neither was, nor had been considered to be essential to the possession of the crown, was proved by the fact of considerable delays having often taken place between the accession of the monarch and his coronation. Henry the Sixth, for instance, was not crowned till eight years after the crown had descended to him. Again, in the "*Pleas of the Crown*," it was held, that the king was fully invested with the crown the moment it descended to him; that he was absolutely king although there should have been no coronation. If the coronation of a king, important as he held it to be, proceeded from the sovereign will, *à fortiori* it must be so with that of a queen-consort. The rights of the queen-consort did not proceed from any coronation; they flowed from her relationship to the sovereign. Her rights were complete and absolute without any coronation. Nor was it essential to the people, for the queen-consort occupied no political station. This view of the right was strengthened by the important preamble of William and Mary, which settled the coronation oath. The language of the act applied to queens regnant, not to queens-consort, for to the latter no oath was administered. As the oath was prescribed, it became necessary that every reigning monarch should be crowned, that there might be the oath and recognition; but the law made no mention of any thing that rendered such a ceremony requisite in the instance of a queen-consort. How then could the crowning of a queen-consort be considered a necessary adjunct of the coronation of the reigning monarch? No part of the ceremony rendered her presence requisite. Selden's work had been quoted in support of the memorial; amongst other things, Selden expressly said that the "anointing, &c. of the queen-consort, were dignities communicated by the king." Selden further stated, that the anointing of the queen, as well as her consecration—it was, in fact, a consecration rather than a coronation—proceeded from the "request" and "demand" of the king, after he had been crowned, made to the metropolitan, who had performed such ceremony. Bracton had entered largely into the particulars *de coronatione regis*, but not one word of the queen's coronation. There was not a single law-writer that had touched upon the existence of such a right, as appertaining to a queen. Blackstone had it not, nor Lord Coke, nor Selden. He next adverted at some length to the precedents quoted by his learned friends opposite, beginning with that of William the Conqueror. The very precedents quoted by his learned friends raised the inference, if there were no other arguments, that the act, so far as related to the queen, was entirely dependent on the will of the king. The Attorney-General then referred largely to Reymer, from whose book he quoted apposite passages, in support of his main argument, that the ceremony of a queen's coronation was entirely dependent upon the order of the king. In all, from the time of Henry the Seventh, six queens had been crowned, and seven had not; so that the majority was against the present claim, which it had been attempted to support on the plea of ancient, uninterrupted usage.

The Attorney-General concluded at a quarter before one o'clock; and the Solicitor-General, after a short pause, rose to follow his learned friend, and of course was compelled to go over the same ground, strengthening and confirming the preceding statements by such arguments as occurred to his observance, and contending that the usage pleaded by her Majesty's law-officers arose entirely from the sovereign's will and pleasure.

About two o'clock Mr. Brougham rose in reply, but we can touch but very briefly on his arguments. It had been intimated that the queen's right to be crowned rested on the proclamation of the king; but it might as well be pleaded that the right of the eldest sons of peers to seats in the House of Lords rested on the king's writ, because usually preceded by it. It had been argued from the word *postulamus*, that the queen's coronation depended on the king's will; but it might as well be argued, from another term employed (*dignemini*), that it was optional in the archbishop. If this right was unnecessary for the queen, how was it necessary to the king? He contended not for the necessity, but the right. The learned gentleman then went over the various cases and authorities of the learned counsel for the crown, and concluded by stating his opinion, that even if the *right* were not established, the expediency was such, that the council would be all but criminal, in advising that her Majesty should be excluded from her part in this important ceremony; for it would be setting an example of the most injurious nature.

Mr. Brougham concluded his reply at half-past three o'clock. Strangers were then ordered to withdraw; the counsel and agents on both sides, however, remaining. The Tower record-keepers were called in, to verify certain documents produced by Mr. Brougham. After which, at a quarter to four o'clock, the Privy Council adjourned.

The decision was ultimately *against* the Queen's claim.

On the 11th of July, in the House of Commons, Mr. Hume made an ineffectual attempt to induce the House to address his Majesty on this much-agitated subject.

He had just commenced the reading of a resolution "That an humble address be presented to his Majesty, praying that he will be graciously pleased to issue his royal proclamation for the coronation of her Majesty," when the deputy-usher of the black rod was heard knocking at the door; and as he was concluding it, he was called to order by the Speaker, who reminded him of the presence of that officer; and proceeded forthwith to the House of Peers, where parliament was prorogued.

The following spirited protest of her Majesty appeared on the 17th.

Her Majesty's Protest Against the Decision of the Privy Council.

Caroline R.

To the King's Most Excellent Majesty.

The Protest and Remonstrance of Caroline, *Queen of Great Britain and Ireland.*

Your Majesty having been pleased to refer to your privy council the Queen's memorial, claiming as of right to celebrate the ceremony of her coronation on the 19th day of July, being the day appointed for the celebration of your Majesty's royal coronation; and Lord Viscount Sidmouth, one of your Majesty's principal secretaries of state, having communicated to the Queen the judgment pronounced against her Majesty's claim; in order to preserve her just rights, and those of her successors, and to prevent the said minute being in after-times referred to as deriving validity from her Majesty's supposed acquiescence in the determination therein expressed, the Queen feels it to be her bounden duty to enter her most deliberate and solemn protest against the said determination; and to affirm and maintain, that by the laws, usages, and customs of this realm, from time immemorial, the queen-consort ought of right to be crowned at the same time with the king's majesty.

In support of this claim of right, her Majesty's law officers have proved before the said council, from the most ancient and authentic records, that queens-consort of this realm have, from time immemorial, participated in the ceremony of the coronation with their royal husbands. The few exceptions that occur demonstrate, from the peculiar circumstances in which they originated, that the right itself was never questioned, though the exercise of it was from necessity suspended, or from motives of policy declined.

Her Majesty has been taught to believe that the most valuable laws of this country depend upon, and derive their authority from, custom; that your Majesty's royal prerogatives stand upon the same basis: the authority of ancient usage cannot therefore be rejected without shaking that foundation upon which the most important rights and institutions of the country depend. Your Majesty's council, however, without controverting any of the facts or reasons upon which the claim made on the part of her Majesty has been supported, have expressed a judgment in opposition to the existence of such right. But the Queen can place no confidence in that judgment, when she recollects that the principal individuals by whom it has been pronounced were formerly her successful defenders; that their opinions have waved with their interest, and that they have since become the most active and powerful of her persecutors: still less can she confide in it, when her Majesty calls to mind that the leading members of that council, when in the service of your Majesty's royal father, reported in the most solemn form, that documents reflecting upon her Majesty were satisfactorily disproved as to the most important parts, and that the remainder was undeserving of credit. Under this declared conviction, they strongly recommended to your Majesty's royal father to bestow his favour upon the Queen, then Princess of Wales, though in opposition to your Majesty's declared wishes. But when your Majesty had assumed the kingly power, these same advisers, in another minute of council, recanted their former judgment, and referred to, and adopted these very same documents as a justification of one of your Majesty's harshest measures towards the Queen—the separation of her Majesty from her affectionate and only child.

The Queen, like your Majesty, descended from a long race of kings, was the daughter of a sovereign house connected by the ties of blood with the most illustrious families in Europe; and her not unequal alliance with your Majesty was formed in full confidence that the faith of the king and the people was equally pledged to secure to her all those honours and rights which had been enjoyed by her royal predecessors.

In that alliance her Majesty believed that she exchanged the protection of her family for that of a royal husband, and that of a free and noble-minded nation. From your Majesty, the Queen has experienced only the bitter disappointment of every hope she had indulged. In the attachment of the people she has found that powerful and decided protection which has ever been her steady support and her unfailing consolation. Submission, from a subject, to injuries of a private nature, may be matter of expedience—from a wife it may be matter of necessity—but it never can be the duty of a queen to acquiesce in the infringement of those rights which belong to her constitutional character.

The Queen does therefore repeat her must solemn and deliberate protest against the decision of the said council, considering it only as the sequel of that course of persecution under which her Majesty has so long and so severely suffered; and which decision, if it is to furnish a precedent for future times, can have no other effect than to fortify oppression with the forms of law, and to give to injustice the sanction of authority. The protection of the subject from the highest to the lowest, is not only the true but the only legitimate object of all power; and no act of power can be legitimate which is not founded on those principles of eternal justice, without which law is but the mask of tyranny, and power the instrument of despotism.

Queen's House, July 17.

On the day of the coronation a considerable crowd assembled about her Majesty's house in South Audley Street soon after four o'clock. As soon as it was ascertained that her Majesty's coach was making ready in the yard, the crowd, both in South Audley Street and in Hill Street, became very great. The wall opposite to her Majesty's house in Hill Street was soon covered with spectators, who announced to the crowd below each successive step of preparation. "The horses are to;" "every thing is quite ready;" "the Queen has entered the coach,"—were the gradual communications, and they were received with the loudest cheers. Lady Anne Hamilton arrived a few minutes before five, and was most cordially and respectfully greeted. Soon after five the gate was thrown open, and a shout was raised—"The Queen! The Queen!" The Queen immediately appeared in her coach of state, drawn by six bays. Lady Hood and Lady Anne Hamilton sat opposite to her Majesty. Lord Hood followed in his own carriage. Her Majesty looked extraordinarily well; and acknowledged, with great dignity and composure, the gratulations of the people on each side of her coach. The course taken was, through Great Stanhope Street, Park Lane, Hyde-Park Corner, the Green Park, St. James's Park, Birdcage Walk, and by Storey's Gate, along Prince's Street, to Dean's Yard—a way, it must be observed, the least likely to attract notice or to gather crowds. The crowd accumulated immensely along this line; the soldiers every where presented arms with the utmost promptitude and respect; and a thousand voices kept up a constant cry of "The Queen!" "The Queen for ever!" The *coup d'œil* from the road along the Green Park, was the most striking which can be imagined; the whole space presented one mass of well dressed males and females hurrying with every possible rapidity to accompany the Queen, and shouting their attachment and admiration. The two torrents that poured along the south side of the park and the eastern end occasioned the greatest conflux at Storey's Gate. As soon as the Queen's arrival was known in the scene of the King's coronation, shouts of "The Queen!" at once arose from all the booths, and hats and handkerchiefs were every where waved in token of respect. As soon as her Majesty came in sight of the coronation platform and Westminster Abbey, she stopped for a few moments, apparently uncertain what course to take, as she had hitherto met with no obstruction, and yet had received nothing like an invitation to approach. At this moment the feelings of the spectators were wound up to a pitch of the most intense curiosity and most painful anxiety. The persons who immediately surrounded her carriage knew no bounds in expressing their enthusiastic attachment, while many of those in the galleries, apprehensive of the consequences of the experiment which she was making, could not restrain their fears and alarms. In the meantime great confusion seemed to prevail among the officers and soldiers on and near the platform; the former giving orders and retracting them, and the latter running to their arms, uncertain whether they should salute her by presenting them or not. Astonishment, hurry, and doubt, seemed to agitate the whole multitude assembled either to witness or compose the ensuing pageant. She alighted from her carriage and proceeded on foot, leaning on the arm of Lord Hood, and accompanied by the faithful companions of her affliction, Lady Hood and Lady Anne Hamilton, to demand admission. The approach of the Queen towards the hall-door produced a considerable sensation within: there was an immediate rush to the door, which was closed amidst much confusion. The officer on guard (we believe Colonel M'Kinnon) was immediately summoned to the spot, and asked her Majesty for her ticket. She replied that she had none, and as Queen of England needed none. He professed his sorrow, but said he must obey orders, and that his orders were to see that no person whatever should be admitted without a ticket. Her Majesty then retired. The party went to the door of the duchy of Lancaster behind the champion's stable, and had the door shut in their faces. They then turned round, and leaving the royal carriage behind, proceeded to demand admission at another entrance. The same intense sensation of interest and the same applause, mixed with partial disapprobation, continued to follow her.

When she arrived nearly at the other extremity of the platform—that which was opposite to the central pavilion—her further progress was arrested by a file of about a dozen soldiers, who were suddenly ordered to form across the platform. Her Majesty then quitted it, and went straight on to the House of Lords on foot, there to repeat the same request, and with the same success.

In about twenty minutes she returned, and having ordered the top of her carriage to be taken down, rode off, amid the astonishment and acclamations of the people.

We subjoin the following account from the *Courier* of her Majesty's reception at the door of Westminster Abbey: —

"Lord Hood having desired admission for her Majesty, the door-keepers drew across the entrance, and requested to see the tickets.

"Lord Hood. — I present you your Queen; surely it is not necessary for her to have a ticket.

"Door-keeper. — Our orders are to admit no person without a peer's ticket.

"Lord Hood. — This is your Queen: she is entitled to admission without such a form.

"The Queen, smiling, but still in some agitation — Yes, I am your Queen, will you admit me?

"Door-keeper. — My orders are specific, and I feel myself bound to obey them.

"The Queen laughed.

"Lord Hood. — I have a ticket.

"Door-keeper. — Then, my Lord, we will let you pass upon producing it.

"Lord Hood now drew from his pocket a peer's ticket for one person; the original name in whose favour it was drawn was erased, and the name of 'Wellington' substituted.

"Door-keeper. — This will let one person pass, but no more.

"Lord Hood. — Will your Majesty go in alone?

"Her Majesty at first assented, but did not persevere,

"Lord Hood.—Am I to understand that you refuse her Majesty admission?

"Door-keeper.—We only act in conformity with our orders.

"Her Majesty again laughed.

"Lord Hood.—Then you refuse the Queen admission?

"A door-keeper of a superior order then came forward, and was asked by Lord Hood whether any preparations had been made for her Majesty? He was answered respectfully in the negative.

"Lord Hood.—Will your Majesty enter the Abbey without your ladies?

"Her Majesty declined.

"Lord Hood then said, that her Majesty had better retire to her carriage. It was clear no provision had been made for her accommodation.

"Her Majesty assented.

"Some persons within the porch of the Abbey laughed, and uttered some expressions of disrespect.

"Lord Hood.—We expected to have met at least with the conduct of gentlemen. Such conduct is neither manly nor mannerly.

"Her Majesty then retired, leaning on Lord Hood's arm, and followed by Lady Hood and Lady Hamilton.

"She was preceded by constables back to the platform, over which she returned, entered her carriage, and was driven off amidst reiterated shouts of mingled applause and disapprobation."

Her Majesty returned through Pall Mall, St. James's Street, and Piccadilly, followed all along by a great concourse of people. In St. James's Street the water had previously created abundance of mud, and this material the crowd bestowed upon some public offices which were prepared for an illumination. During the whole course of her Majesty's progress no accident occurred.

Footnotes:

[1] See Toland; Sir J. Ware's Antiq. of Ireland, vol. ii. pp. 10, 124, &c.

[2] Called also by the Irish Cloch na cineaṁna, or, the Stone of Fortune.

[3] History of the Druids, p. 104.

[4] Chron. of Scotland, lib. i. cap. 2.

[5] P. 54.

[6] Judges ix. 6.

[7] 2 Kings, xi. 12, 14.

[8] Taylor's Glory of Regality, p. 31.

[9] Richard III.

[10] In the Archæologia, vol. xv. art. 24, is "A true and perfect Inventory of all the Plate and Jewells now being in the Upper Jewell House of the Tower, in the charge of Sir Henry Mildmay, together with an appraisement of them, made and taken the 13th, 14th, and 15th daies of August, 1649;" containing the following account of "crowns," &c. demolished:—

	£.	s.	d.
"The imperiall crowne of massy gold, weighing 7 lb. 6 oz. valued at	1110	0	0
The queene's crowne of massy gold, weighing 3 lb. 10 oz.	338	3	4

A small crowne found in an iron chest formerly in the Lord Cottingham's charge, &c.:

The gold	73	16	8
The diamonds, rubies, sapphires, &c.	355	0	0
The globe, weighing 1 lb. 5¼ oz.	57	10	0
Two coronation bracelets, weighing 7 oz. (with three rubies and twelve pearls)	36	0	0
Two sceptres, weighing 11 oz.	60	0	0
A long rod of silver gilt, 1 lb. 5 oz.	4	10	8

"The foremencion'd crownes, since the inventorie was taken, are, according to ordr of Parliamt, totallie broken and defaced."

A second inventory, containing "that part of the regalia" found at Westminster, mentions "King Alfred's crowne of gould wyer worke, sett with slight stones, and 2 little bells, p. oz. 79½, at £3. per oz., £248. 10*s*. 0*d*."

[11] See Sir Edward Walker's Account of "The Preparations for His Majesty's Coronation," &c. 8vo. Lond. First printed 1820.

[12] Taylor, p, 65. The Saxon Chronicle says of the Conqueror: "He was very worshipful. Thrice he bore his *king-helmet* every year, when he was in England: at Easter, he bore it at Winchester; at Pentecost, at Westminster; in midwinter, at Gloucester. And there were with him all the rich men over all England," &c. — *Sax. Chron.* 189, &c.

[13] The following is Hume's account of this memorable project: —

"A little after [his attempt to carry off the Duke of Ormond], Blood formed a design of carrying off the crown and regalia from the Tower; a design to which he was prompted, as well by the surprising boldness of the enterprise, as by the views of profit. He was near succeeding; he had bound and wounded Edwards, the keeper of the Jewel Office, and had gotten out of the Tower with his prey; but was overtaken and seized, with some of his associates. One of them was known to have been concerned in the attempt upon Ormond; and Blood was immediately concluded to be the ring-leader. When questioned, he frankly avowed the enterprise, but refused to tell his accomplices. 'The fear of death,' he said, 'should never engage him either to deny a guilt, or betray a friend.' All these extraordinary circumstances made him the general subject of conversation; and the king was moved by an idle curiosity to see and speak with a person so noted for his courage and his crimes.... Blood might now esteem himself secure of pardon, and he wanted not address to improve the opportunity." — Charles eventually pardoned him, granted him an estate of £500. per annum, and encouraged his attendance about his person. "And while old Edwards, who had bravely ventured his life, and had been wounded in defending the crown and regalia, was forgotten and neglected, this man, who deserved only to be stared at and detested as a monster, became a kind of favourite." — Hume's *England*, Charles II.

[14] Gen. xlix. 10.

[15] Sandford does not omit to notice, that the dean of Westmin-

ster, assisted by the prebendaries, duly performed this office for the coronation of James II., "early in the morning."

[16] Vide Judges, chap. ix.

[17] Titles of Honour, p. i, chap. 8.

[18] 1 Sam. x. 10; xvi. 1; 1 Kings, xiv. 15; &c.

[19] 1 Sam. xxvi. 9, 10.

[20] Selden's Titles.

[21] Marmion, 8vo. Note, p. 456.

[22] "Comite Cestriæ gladium S. Edwardi, qui *Curtein* dicetur, ante regem bagulante," &c.

[23] Glory of Regality, p. 73, 4.

[24] Esther, iii. 10, and viii. 2.

[25] Golden Legende (Julyan Notary, 1503).

[26] Battley's Antiq. St. Edm. Burgi, p. 119.

[27] Memoirs of James II., ed. by Clarke. 2 vols, 4to.

[28] Rot. Parl. iii. 417.

[29] Lingard's Hist. England, iii. p. 51.

[30] Strutt's Horda Angel-cẏnnan, v. ii.

[31] Glory of Regality, p. 81.

[32] These were (prudently enough, after the error hinted at,) the whole of the words used at the late ceremonial.

[33] Being first given by Sandford to his description of this part of the ceremony of James II.'s coronation.

[34] Doleman's Conferences concerning Succession, &c.

[35] MS. Cott. Nero, c. ix. p. 172.

[36] See his curious Speech in M. Paris, Hist. Major, 1640, p. 197.

[37] Hoveden, Walsingham, &c. are quoted to this effect by Taylor.

[38] History of the Anglo-Saxons, b. iv. chap. 1.

[39] Titles of Honour, p. ii. c. v. 26.

[40] Wharton's Troubles of Archbishop Laud, p. 324.

[41] Inserted on the union with Scotland, in 1707.

[42] In the oath recently taken by His Majesty the latter members of this clause, read 'within England and Ireland, and the territories thereunto belonging.'

[43] Stow's Annals.

[44] In France we read of the exaltation of king Pharamond on a shield, so early as the year 420; of the chairing of Gunbald, king of Burgundy, A.D. 500, in which that prince fell from the supporting arms of his subjects, nearly to the ground; and of king Pepin being elevated on a target in 751. (Greg. Turon. Hist. lib. vii. cap. 10. Mezeray Hist. de Pepin, &c.) In Navarre, the king and queen, after being anointed, were thrice elevated before the altar on a shield emblazoned with the arms of the kingdom, and upheld by six staves.

[45] Thus in the ordo of Henry VII.'s coronation; "the cardinal," it is said, "sitting, shall anoynte the king, kneeling." — Ive's *Papers*.

[46] Vide Taylor's Additional Notes, p. 347, &c.

[47] It will complete the sketch of the history of an institution closely connected with our subject, to observe, that George I. on restoring it in 1725, constituted it a regular military order of thirty-six companions and one grand-master, having as officers a dean, genealogist, king at arms, register, secretary, usher and messenger; and a seal, on one side of which is the figure of the king on horseback in complete armour, the shield azure and three imperial crowns with the circumscription, *Sigillum Honoratissimi Militaris Ordinis De Balneo*; and on the reverse the same, impaling the royal arms.

The badge of the order exhibits a happy specimen of the art of moulding old institutions to modern purposes. It consists of a rose, thistle and shamrock, issuing from a sceptre surrounded by three imperial crowns, enclosed within the ancient motto *Tria juncta in uno*. Of pure gold chased and pierced, it is worn by the knight elect pendant from a red riband across the right shoulder. The collar is also of gold, weighing thirty ounces troy, and is composed of nine imperial crowns, and eight roses, thistles, and shamrocks, issuing from a sceptre, enamelled in proper colours, tied or linked together with seventeen gold knots, enamelled white, and having the badge of the order pendant from it. The star consists of three imperial crowns of gold, surrounded by the motto upon a circle of red, with rays issuing from the silver centre forming a star, and is embroidered on the left side of the upper garment.

The installation dress is a surcoat of white satin, a mantle of crimson satin lined with white, tied at the neck with a cordon of crimson silk and gold, with gold tassels, and the star of the order embroidered on the left shoulder; a white silk hat adorned with a standing plume of white ostrich feathers, white leather boots, edged and heeled, spurs of crimson and gold, a sword in a white leather scabbard with cross hilts of gold. Each knight is allowed three squires, who must be gentlemen of blood, bearing coat armour, and who are entitled during life to all the privileges and exemptions enjoyed by the esquires of the sovereign's body, or the gentlemen of the privy chamber.

We need hardly add, that both in the number of knights and the brilliancy of its appearance, this order maintained its full splendor at the coronation of the fourth sovereign of the House of Brunswick.

[48] Johnes' Froissart, v. 12. p. 160, 1.

[49] King Richard II.

[50] Rot. Parl, vi. 278.

[51] Lingard's History of England, v. iii. p. 662, 3.

[52] Ives' Coronacion of Queene Elizabeth, p. 120.

[53] Ives' Coronacion of Queene Elizabeth, p. 120.

[54] Hall's Chronicle.

[55] Hall's Chronicle, Henry VIII.

[56] There have been instances in which the see having been vacant, and the archbishop suspended or abroad, other prelates have officiated: but the right of the metropolitan see seems to have been still preserved.

[57] Lingard's History of England, vol. ii. p. 88, 89.

[58] Henry V. p. i.

[59] Johnes' Froissart, v. 12. p. 162.

[60] Chron. Sax. 57, 63; Malmsbury, &c.

[61] Wilk. Leg. 217, 228.

[62] Ivanhoe, v. iii. p. 328-345.

[63] Gen. xli. 9.

[64] Neh. i. 11.

[65] Clarke's Bible, Part ii. Exod.

[66] Hist. Anglo-Saxons, v. ii, p. 79.

[67] Malmsb. lib. iii. p. 80.

[68] The beautiful anecdote which Mr. Lingard furnishes from Bede of the debate on the conversion of the Northumbrian king, *Edwin*, we cannot forbear transcribing. The high priest of the heathen rites having spoken—a thane "sought for information respecting the origin and destiny of man. 'Often,' said he, 'O king, in the depth of winter, while you are feasting with your thanes, and the fire is blazing on the hearth in the midst of the hall, you have seen a bird, pelted by the storm, enter at one door, and escape at the other. During its passage it was visible: but whence it came, or whither it went, you knew not. Such to me appears the life of man. He walks the earth for a few years: but what precedes his birth, or what is to follow after death, we cannot tell. Undoubtedly, if the new religion can unfold these important secrets, it must be worthy our attention.'"—*Lingard's History*, vol. i. p. 92.

[69] The see of Canterbury was restored to the primacy again by Cenulf, the successor of Egfurth.

[70] Ep. Car. Mag. ap. Bouquet, tom. v. p. 260.

[71] Titles of Honour, p. i. chap. 1.

[72] See Mr. Turner's Anglo-Saxons, Spelman's Life of Alfred, &c.

[73] Taylor's Glory of Regality, Addit. Notes, p. 310.

[74] Lingard's History, vol. i. p. 350.

[75] See Hume's England, 8vo. vol. i. &c.

[76] Turner's Anglo-Saxons, 4to. vol. i. p. 389.

[77] "Princes beyond the baths of the sea-fowl, worshipped him far and wide," says a poem on his death: "they bowed to the king as one of their own kin. There was no fleet so proud, there was no host so strong, as to seek food in England, while this noble king ruled the kingdom. He reared up God's honour, he loved God's law, he preserved the people's peace; the best of all the kings that were before in the memory of man. And God was his helper: and kings and earls bowed to him: and they obeyed his will: and without battle he ended all as he willed." — *Chron. Sax.* p. 122.

[78] Osbern, 113. Eadmer, 220.

[79] Mr. Lingard has the following note on the accession of Edwy, confirming our previous observations on the meaning of the recognition. "It is observable, that the ancient writers almost always speak of our kings as *elected*. Edwy's grandmother in her charter, (Lye, App. iv.) says, "He was chosen, *gecoren*." The contemporary biographer of Dunstan, (apud Boll. tom. iv. Maii, 344.) says, "Ab universis Anglorum principibus communi electione.""

[80] Hickes' Inst. Gram. Præf.

[81] Lingard's Hist. p. 292.

[82] Thus the Saxon Chronicler says of William I. "Thrice he bore his *king-helmet* every year, when he was in England; at Easter he bore it at Winchester, at Pentecost at Westminster, and in Midwinter at Gloucester." p. 450.

[83] We have noticed the present existence of a contemporary account of the coronation of Ethelred II. It demonstrates, that

some of the most eloquent passages of the prayers now used on the occasion, were the production of what we often denominate the darker ages of the world, and well accords with the preceding sketch of the character and duties of the Saxon kings.

"Two bishops, with the witan [A]," it is said, "shall lead the king to church; and the clergy with the bishops shall sing the anthem, *Firmetur manus tua*, and the *Gloria Patri*. When the king arrives at the church, he shall prostrate himself before the altar, and the *Te Deum* shall be chanted. When this is finished, the king shall be raised from the ground, and having been *chosen* by the bishops and people, shall with a clear voice, before God and all the people, promise that he will observe these three rules." [Then follows the coronation oath, quoted above.]

[A] MS. Claude, A. 3. Cotton Library.

The prayers that follow, the bishops shall separately repeat. "We invoke thee, O Lord, Holy Father Almighty and Eternal God, that this thy servant, whom by the wisdom of thy divine dispensations from the beginning of his existence to this day, thou hast permitted to increase, rejoicing in the flower of youth, enriched with the gift of thy piety, and full of the grace of thy truth, thou mayest cause to be always advancing, day by day, to better things before God and men; — that rejoicing in the bounty of supernal grace, he may receive the throne of supreme power; and, defended on all sides from his enemies by the wall of thy mercy, he may deserve to govern happily the people committed to him, with the peace of propitiation and the strength of victory."

The following combination of admirable Scripture allusions is extracted from the third prayer, or that offered by the bishop after the consecration, "holding the crown over the king."

"Almighty Creator, everlasting Lord, Governor of heaven and earth, the Maker and Disposer of angels and men, King of kings and Lord of lords! who made thy faithful servant Abraham to triumph over his enemies, and gavest manifold victories to Moses and Joshua, the *prelates* of thy people; and didst raise David, thy lowly child, to the summit of the kingdom, and didst free him from the mouth of the lion and the paws of the bear, and from

Goliath, and from the malignant sword of Saul; who didst endow Solomon with the ineffable gift of wisdom and peace;—look down propitiously on our humble prayers, and multiply the gifts of thy blessing on this thy servant, whom with humble devotion we have chosen to be king of the Angles and Saxons. Surround him everywhere with the right hand of thy power, that, strengthened with the faith of Abraham, the meekness of Moses, the courage of Joshua, the humility of David, and the wisdom of Solomon, he may be well pleasing to thee in all things, and may always advance in the way of justice with inoffensive progress."

When crowned, the invocation is, "May God crown thee with the honour of justice, and the labour of fortitude; that by the virtue of *our* benediction, and by a right faith, and the various fruit of good works, thou mayest attain to the crown of the everlasting kingdom, through his bounty whose kingdom endureth for ever!"

We cannot omit the concluding benedictions, rich with Scripture phraseology as any church could make them.

"May the Almighty Lord give thee, from the dew of heaven, and the fatness of the earth, abundance of corn, wine, and oil! May the people serve thee, and the tribes adore thee! Be the lord of thy brothers, and let the sons of thy mother bow before thee! He who blesses thee shall be filled with blessings; for God will be thy helper. May the Almighty bless thee with the blessings of the heaven above, and in the mountains and the valleys; with the blessings of the deep below; with the blessings of the suckling and the womb; with the blessings of grapes and apples; and may the blessing of the ancient fathers, Abraham, Isaac, and Jacob, be heaped upon thee!—May the blessing of Him, who appeared in the bush, come upon his head, and may the full blessing of the Lord be upon his sons, and may he steep his feet in oil! With his horn, as the horn of the rhinoceros, may he push the nations to the extremities of the earth; and may He who has ascended the skies be his auxiliary for ever!"

[84] Chron. Sax. 257.

[85] Lingard, vol. i. 485.

[86] A tax of two shillings per hide on land, gathered annually.

[87] History of England, 8vo. edit. vol. i. p. 413.

[88] Holinshed.

[89] This is the common statement: Mr. Taylor (Glory of Regality, p. 249,) objects to this being considered as a second coronation, and thinks it only a renewal of the royal festivities at Easter, with unusual splendor. But he seems to overlook the formal resolve of the council at Nottingham, on the point.

[90] See the whole speech, in Matt. Paris.

[91] Leg. Sex. 154.

[92] Brompton, 1283, 4.

[93] See M. Paris, Rymer, &c.

[94] Holinshed.

[95] The queen is said to have sucked the poison out of a wound which her husband received in the Holy Land, from the poisoned dagger of the emir of Jaffa. — See Lingard, v. ii. p. 369.

[96] Johnes' Froissart, i. xxv.

[97] Rymer, vii.

[98] Rot. Parl. iii.

[99] See the curious original document in Hume.

[100] King Henry IV. p. ii.

[101] See a curious MS. account of this 'solempnyte' in the Cotton Library, as quoted by Mr. Taylor, Glory of Regality, p. 263.

[102] See the preceding Note.

[103] Grafton, vol i. p. 592.

[104] Historic Doubts, Lord Orford's Works, 5 vols. 4to. vol. ii. p. 146.

[105] Grafton, vol. ii. p. 156.

[106] Burnet on the Reformation, and Appendix.

[107] Walker's Circumstantial Account, 8vo. 1. p. 78.

[108] Taylor's Preface, p. x.

[109] Page 37.

[110] No. 335. — The Spectator's encomium on Booth is, however, sufficiently slight. The good bishop, it is evident, was better acquainted with the realities he was here describing than these theatrical types.

[111] Here the archbishop took the paten into his hands.

[112] And here broke the bread.

[113] Here the archbishop laid his hand upon all the bread.

[114] Here he took the cup into his hand.

[115] And here laid his hand upon every vessel (be it chalice or flagon) in which there was any wine to be consecrated.

The End.

www.ingramcontent.com/pod-product-compliance
Lightning Source LLC
Chambersburg PA
CBHW021405290426
44108CB00010B/400